HOW TO CLIMB
THE MOUNTAIN OF
FINANCIAL AID

By

Trae D. Johnson

CAMPANIA PUBLISHING, LLC

2021 Edition

CAMPANIA PUBLISHING, LLC

How to Climb the Mountain of Financial Aid
Copyright 2021
Trae D. Johnson

This book is a work of non-fiction and is based on the author's experience. Neither Campania Publishing, LLC nor Trae D. Johnson is giving financial advice because neither is a Certified Public Accountant nor a financial attorney. This book is for educational purposes only. It is created to provide information on financial aid, loans, and college life. It is sold with the understanding that the author, publisher, and Campania Publishing, LLC are not engaged in providing legal, accounting, or any other professional services. If you need an expert in legal or accounting matters, a competent, knowledgeable professional should be contacted. The purpose of this book is to enlighten, educate, and entertain. A strong effort has been made to make sure that the information in this book is accurate and complete. This book should be used as a basic guide to understanding, navigating and conquering the financial aid process. The author encourages you to read and research all aspects of financial aid, loans, colleges, and various scholarships and grants that may also assist students in college expenses.

Publisher: Campania Publishing, LLC
Editor: Sarah Vaughan
Cover Design: Rebeccacovers

Printed in the United States of America. All Rights Reserved. No part of this publication may be reproduced in any form or by any means, including scanning, photocopying, or otherwise without prior written permission of the copyright holder. Contact author at Campaniapublishing@gmail.com or www.traejohnson.com.

Library of Congress Cataloging-in-Publication Data
Johnson, Trae D.
How to Climb the Mountain of Financial Aid/Trae D. Johnson p. com.
ISBN-13: 978-1-7355266-2-1
1. Self-help   2. Education

0 1 2 3 4 5 6 7 8 9

WHAT ARE PEOPLE SAYING ABOUT THIS BOOK?

"Trae provides realistic examples that are relatable to any audience. This book is a great resource for educators, students, and parents, but I believe that first generation college students would be especially prepared for the financial aid process by simply reading this book. The financial aid process can be daunting at times but this book will put your mind at ease."
–Daisha Levy, High School Counselor

"It has been said that success is born when preparation meets opportunity. "How to Climb the Mountain of Financial Aid" is an exceptional resource for students and parents that gives a road map on how to navigate through the financial aid process. Mr. Johnson gives students a great opportunity to be fully prepared for success by building a financial game plan for college!"
- Dr. Terrie Lockhart, NBCT (National Board Certified Teacher)

"I wish you had written this book before I started college. The language you use is easy to follow and not above my head. I would purchase this as a gift for a student headed to college. I teach math at a community college, and students often ask financial aid questions even though this is not my area. Reading this book can help me provide better responses to their questions."
- Quillie Hunt, Jr., College Mathematics Instructor

Table of Contents

Acknowledgment vi
Preface viii
Introduction x

Chapter 1
   Preparing to Make the Hike 1

Chapter 2
   Family Educational Rights and Privacy Act (FERPA) 13

Chapter 3
   Knowing the Right Equipment 17

Chapter 4
   Preparing for the Mountain of Financial Aid 29

Chapter 5
   Dependent vs. Independent 37

Chapter 6
   FAFSA Aftermath 39

Chapter 7
   Estimated Family Contribution (EFC) 47

Chapter 8
   Loans 55

Chapter 9
   Seasons of Financial Aid 66

Chapter 10
  Satisfactory Academic Progress (SAP) 76
Chapter 11
  What is a Financial Aid Appeal? 81
Chapter 12
  Parent and Child (Student) Relationship 87
Chapter 13
  International Students 94
Chapter 14
  Top of the Mountain 96
Chapter 15
  Key Terms 100
References 107
About the Author 108

Acknowledgment

First, I thank God for all of his blessings and helping me to fulfill my dream as an author and entrepreneur. Campania Publishing, LLC is no longer a thought or a dream, it's a reality!

I thank my wife, LaToya B. Johnson, for her love and support. I want to give a Big Shout Out to my support team: thank you Dad - Jimmie Johnson, Taryon Johnson, TaVonda and Robert L. Collins, Sallie and Preston "PAP" Bentley. Thank you to my manager Eric D. Smith - I appreciate your support. Thank you to Virgil L. Dortch III, Dr. Corey Stayton, David Reed, and Tony Ellison for always having my back. Thank you to Dr. Mary O'Connor. Thank you for your encouragement to write this book. Thank you to all the educators who supported me in writing this book. Thank you Lee Ashby Watts for your marketing expertise. Thank you Ken G. Love for your inspiration and support. Thank you Dr. Mel Caudle for your support. Thank you Sandra Turner for your support and wise council. Thank you Brittne Ballenger-Jackson, Esq. for your legal counsel. Thank you to Sedrick Strickland for opening the doors for me in the financial aid industry. Thank you to LaTonja Parker and Brandon Burton for your leadership. Thank you Mrs. Janiece Howard for your unwavering support. Eli Duval, thank you for your help and encouragement. Thank you to Sarah Vaughan, my editor, and Rebeccacovers for designing the book cover. Thank you to my Focus Group: Tociana "Love" Watley, MSW, LCSW-A, Angela D. Duncan, PhD, and Contessa Paige.

Thank you to everyone who prayed for me. Thank you to all who have purchased this book and supported Campania Publishing, LLC. Thank you so much! I hope that you find this book to be helpful and educational. Finally, I want to give a Big Heavenly Shout Out to my mother, Essie L. Johnson and my Granny, Moriah Johnson. I wish you two were here to see this dream come true. Only God knows how much I missed you.

With Love,

Trae D. Johnson

Preface

When I shared with a few people that I was thinking of writing a book about financial aid and college life, I was told "Finally!", "Hallelujah!", "Can't Wait!", and "It's Needed!" With my 10 years of financial aid and higher education experience, I've seen many things that could have been avoided if someone had said something. I often think about my undergraduate college journey and think about the things that I wish I should have done or could have done. For example, was this the best college fit for me? I can sit back and think about it, but nothing can change my past; however, I may be able to help students who are eager to learn but naive in the process of applying to and getting through college like I was.

Working with students, parents, guardians, faculty, and staff has been a journey. Depending on the situation, it has even felt like an adventure sometimes. One of my greatest joys is seeing a student, who was lost and nervous when they first came in, or as they say in the country "wet behind the ears," finally walk across the stage, getting their degree and ready for the world!

I hope this book will give you some helpful advice and insight on college life. Be aware that college is a business. Let me say this once again, college is a business. If college is a business, then you need to look at yourself as a valuable customer or stakeholder. With any business deals, both sides have a responsibility. Not only does each side have a responsibility to maximize their potential but both sides should have a clear understanding of each other.

When you read this book, I want you to feel as if you were in my office, sitting across from me, knowing that you have someone who wants you to succeed and is giving you some "Keep It Real" advice.

Introduction

Before the world changed in 2020, right before the start of each semester, students and their parents or guardians would wait in the lobby of my office, anxious to discuss their financial aid status. Many students and parents could not wait to voice their concerns, return a document, complain, or have their questions answered. I never understood why a student would say, "I have a quick question," when that's normally never the case.

At times, dealing with financial aid is like trying to climb a mountain but without any training or equipment. This situation led me to wonder "why isn't there a practical manual to educate students, parents/guardians, and in some cases, faculty and staff to unlock the mysteries of financial aid?"

In case you are wondering who I am, my name is Trae D. Johnson. My background includes ten years of financial aid experience at a college and before that I was a student loan debt collector. I worked for a state college and a private for-profit college. I've done financial aid outreach programs for high schools, explained to international students about financial aid and how to get into college, sat on a panel to discuss admissions and financial aid, conducted financial aid workshops with church groups, and with non-profit organizations. I have worked with higher education departments such as Enrollment and Registration, Student Accounts, Cashier, Student Affairs, and the Dean's Office. I have invited faculty and staff from various departments to come and see me if they have questions or concerns about financial aid. Often they come because of an issue with one of their students, which then becomes a learning experience for them. In 2015 I received the Student Financial Services Outstanding Counselor of the Year Award.

Now that you know a little of my background and understand that I have extensive financial aid and higher education experience, let me get to the nitty gritty of why you are opening this book. I am the author of "How to Climb the Mountain of Financial Aid." I can only guess that you have purchased this book, skimmed over it to see if it would be beneficial to you, or are simply curious to know about financial aid and what to expect.

Whatever your reasons, I want you to see yourself in every aspect of this book. Over the years I have noticed that there are several types of students that a financial aid rep might serve. Below are a few names and descriptions that I created. Which one(s) are you?

The Always on Time Student: This student completed their Free Application for Federal Student Aid (FAFSA) three months ago and just wants to know their status.

The Procrastinator: The person who waits until the last minute to get everything done.

The Excuser: This person makes excuses for everything - from the reason why they have not completed their FAFSA to why they are not turning in their assignments.

> ***The difference between the Procrastinator and Excuser is the Procrastinator will admit their error and accept if things do not work in their favor.*

The Assumer: This type of person assumes that everything was done correctly. They do not go back to check if everything is correct until they receive a notification from the college that they were selected for verification and various documents are missing.

The Newbies: Newbies are those who are attending college for the very first time. Some may think that newbies are only recent high school graduates; however, Newbies include anyone who is starting school for the first time.

First Generation: Neither parent completed a four-year degree.

The Seasoned Student: This student is one who has been in school for quite a while or who has been in school so long that they actually wonder if they will ever graduate. The seasoned student often thinks they know it all.

Mama Knows It Student: This is the type of student that has their Mama do all the paperwork for admittance and financial aid. The student has no clue of what's going on regarding his/her admission or financial aid status. This student's mother often gets upset when she comes to the office and wants to speak about their child's account, but is not allowed to because of a law called FERPA - Family Educational Rights and Privacy Act.

If you are the first person in your family who is going to college, you should be planning to do as much research as you can since you do not have anyone in your inner circle who has gone to college to advise you. Throughout my ten years of financial aid experience from state university to private for- profit school, I have found three key points that everyone needs to know. (1) College is a business (2) Always expect change and (3) Financial Aid can be very intimidating. Why can't learning about financial aid be simple and easy? There are "how to" books on how to learn Parliamentary Procedures and Calculus. Why is something so important so difficult to understand?

In this book, I try to make navigating financial aid simple and understandable for those who are attending college for the first time or those who are returning to college and need more of an understanding of what this FAFSA "stuff" really means. Many of the processes from 20 years ago are not relevant today. I want to wipe away your fears about financial aid. This book is to help you learn the basics of financial aid. Wait... let's not think of this as a book! Think of it as a cheat sheet, a map, and an insider's guide. Better still, think of it as a mountain you will prepare for, climb and conquer!

Enjoy,
Trae D. Johnson

Chapter 1

Preparing to Make the Hike

"I can't wait to grow up, so I can do what I wanna do!"

As you begin reading "How to Climb the Mountain of Financial Aid," there is a personal message I would like to share with students, parents, and their support system. I hope that you will take this message to heart because I truly want you to succeed and to fulfill your educational and career goals. As stated in my introduction, I have ten years of financial aid experience, and within those years, I have witnessed the same scenarios over and over again. It has almost become a movie or play, the same storyline but with different characters.

Students

To the students who are saying: *"I'm trying to figure out what should I do?"*

For those students who are still in high school, continue to work hard and strive for the best. It would not be long until you order your cap and gown, and begin the countdown to the down you graduate from high school.

To those students who have graduated from high school, congratulations! Congrats for graduating high school and taking your talents to the next level! You worked hard, stayed focused and dedicated and you were able to earn that diploma. Like food and water are critical for our survival, a good education is vital to functioning in society. From learning U.S Government, understanding how to properly write (not text), and figuring out how important it is to add, subtract, tell time, and count money, education is extremely important. Like anything else in life, you cannot do it by yourself. If you have not already, please take the time to tell your parent/guardian and all the people who helped you "Thank You". Whether you know it or not, they sacrificed a great deal for you. Their love, dedication, time, money, nerves, and energy helped to mold you into the person you are today. I can't tell you how many times I have thanked my parents. So... at this moment, please tell your parent(s) or guardian(s) THANK YOU. It was a long road, but you did it!

Now you have entered a new chapter in your life called "The Real World." All of those life skills that your parents taught you and those experiences that you learned will now be used and tested. You will quickly learn that college is not high school. Mom and Dad can't always save you. They can support you but now it's time to be fully responsible for your actions. While you are attending college to educate yourself for a future career, you will also be developing your networking skills and hopefully, hanging with like-minded people. Your college years should be some of the best years of your life. With that being said, we don't expect you to party all 4-5 years. The key focus is your goals and how you are going to accomplish them.

As this new chapter opens in your life, you must ask yourself some tough questions. For example, do you really want to go to college? Are you going to college because your parents demanded you to? Do you have an idea of what you want to major in? What are your career goals? These questions are important because many times students do something that they believe is what they are "supposed to do" or because they do not want to disappoint someone, like a parent. In time, you will realize that your heart is not in it and this results in failing grades and loss of financial aid. So before you make a move, know where you want to go. Trust me, I have spoken to students who regret not getting their degree or not taking college seriously in their early 20's. Now they are in their 40's, wishing they could have received their degree before their spouse or children came into the picture.

Parents/ Guardians

To the parents/guardians who have often asked: "So... what are your plans after high school?"

To you I say "Congratulations!" For 18-19 years, you worked hard in raising your child (the student), educating them on the rights and wrongs in life, and even sacrificing things you needed for yourself in order to provide for your child. I am not a father yet but I've seen my god- sister raise her twins, witnessed other parents raising their children, and listened to parents in my office discussing what they dealt with while raising their child. It's not an easy job, and I commend you!

With all the good that you have accomplished, there are some parents who have done some things that hurt their child's growth into adulthood- such as not letting your child take on their own responsibilities without you always trying to save them. Many times I have witnessed a parent coming in, trying to take care of all the students' admission and financial aid responsibilities. When I ask where the student is many parents respond, "at home sleeping!" This leaves me to wonder, does the student really want to go to school or they are forced to go by the parent?

Do you know why the mama bird pushes her young out of the nest? If she didn't, the young bird would feel comfortable just lying in the nest and having the mother provide for it. Pushing the young bird out of the nest will force it to learn to fly and to survive. Too many times I have seen a parent who is doing everything for the child. How can a child learn how to be responsible if you as a parent are always doing everything for them? It's really an eye opener when some of my college professor friends tell me that their student's parents call or email them to see if their child can get another chance on a paper or report. Most of them tell the parents that it is their child's responsibility to make such a call and will ask them to tell their child to start coming to class.

Parents, I understand that you want the best for your child; however, your child must want the best for themselves. Supporting your child is great! I encourage that! But doing all their work and taking on their responsibilities helps to create a lazy student.

Support System

"So, what do you think I should do?"

Students, pay attention to the people who support and encourage you- teachers, mentors, church friends, family members, and neighbors. Typically your support systems are the really close friends that you tell your biggest secrets, have the most conversations, or who give you advice on matters that you may not feel comfortable talking about with your parents.

Your support systems are important because there will be times when you may want to quit or there may be something derailing your efforts to pursue your dreams. A true support system will uplift you and certainly will encourage you. They will work with you in trying to solve your problems. They are GREAT FRIENDS! Just think, when you were in high school, they were the friends who listened to you when you talked about that girl/guy that you really liked and tried to motivate you to speak with her/him. Your close friends are also the ones who told you to never give up - like that good teammate who wants to see you succeed because they know that you deserve it. Besides your parents, your support systems are your biggest cheerleaders!

A support systems' responsibility has not changed. Such a person is still a vital piece of the student's life. There may be times that the student wants to quit school, but you encourage them to stay. College is a new chapter in their life, so having that dependable and reliable friend is important. A true support system can also be that friend who will not hesitate to watch out for the student when the student feels that his or her life is spiraling down and no one understands.

Women-who often hear

"So, when you get your degree, I know you're going to leave me!"

I wanted to make sure to address this common deterrent because I hope that I can inspire someone not to let go of their dreams because of someone else. Though my main audience for this section is women, fathers... I need you to read this as well and make sure that you instill this in your daughters... "Don't Let A Man Discourage You from Getting an Education."

Financial Aid representatives often have a rapport with students and many times students will open up to them. There have been many times when a female student would excitingly let me know that she studied for weeks, made huge sacrifices, did not socialize, but just studied all the time, or how she would stay in a coffee shop for hours just to read several chapters of an assignment. The joy of getting that "A" was just as thrilling as climbing up the top of a mountain and planting that flag on the top. You would think that her spouse or significant other would be just as happy to hear the great news that she was so elated to share with me. Sadly; however, they are not. Several women have told me that their significant other hates the fact that they are in school and actively discourages them from continuing their studies. For example, they may claim that someone (the female student) needs to be home to help their child/children with their homework, cook dinner, or they might say the family cannot afford to have a parent go to school even if the female students have the Pell Grant at a community college that pays for their tuition and books (especially if they are an in-state student).

One of the laughable, low self-esteem comments I've heard is a man who said to his significant other that when she receives an education, she would leave him or think that she is better than him! An education is a tool that cannot only unlock your mind but can also offer you a career that can take you many places. Ladies, if your man does not support you in improving yourself with an education, you may want to consider changing your man. There are too many educated and talented women who deprive themselves of an education by listening to an unsupportive significant other.

You vs. Life

"Yeah I can handle working 40 hours a week and going to school fulltime! I gotta hurry up and get this degree!"

College is a life- changing, transformative experience! Many undergraduate students would say that their college years were the greatest years of their lives. After college, students want to know if it was worth obtaining that degree.

Consider this: Over a lifetime, individuals with a Bachelor's degree:

- Make 84% more than those with only a high school diploma. (per Georgetown's Center on Education and the Workforce)

- Earn an average of 63% more in hourly wages than those with only a high school diploma. (per College Board Advocacy and Policy Center)

- Earn an average of $22,000 more per year than those with only a high school diploma. (per College Board Advocacy and Policy Center)

I have had many returning students come into my office, full of excitement and ready to get back and tackle college. While reviewing their financial aid status, the student would mention to me about their past and how they were not focused on college at first but since they had a taste of the real world, they are much more focused and want to get back into college. As I'm reviewing their past grades, and poor GPA, I say to myself, "Yeah, you definitely were not focused!"

When they finish telling me their story, I inform them that their financial aid has been denied and explain the reason to them. I usually get one of two responses. (1) "Oh… I had a feeling it was denied. I was suspended for a year due to my academics. So, what's your payment plan option?" The other response is: What? That happened so long ago… come on?" My response is to explain to them Satisfactory Academic Progress (SAP). Let me explain to them SAP.

There are three main reasons why students lose their financial aid (which we will discuss in Chapter 10), but there is a fourth reason that is rarely discussed because many people think that they can handle it. They believe it is not an issue that they or others should worry about! That reason would be "life." When I say life,

I am not speaking of your life expectancy. I am referring to everything that you have going on in your world that would compete such as college activities like homework, tests, or group projects. It could be your child's school activities, illness or death of a family member or friend, church events, a sick child, your own illness, your financial situation, job, or anything that could cause you to lose your focus on your educational goals.

Let us look at this example: You are a full-time student (typically taking a minimum of 12 credit hours or 4 classes per semester). Let's say that you are taking the following classes this semester: English 101, College Algebra, World History, Chemistry, and Chemistry Lab. You need to be in class for 12 hours each week and can expect 1-3 hours of homework per class per week.

24 hours in a day X 5 Days a Week= 120 hours in a work week

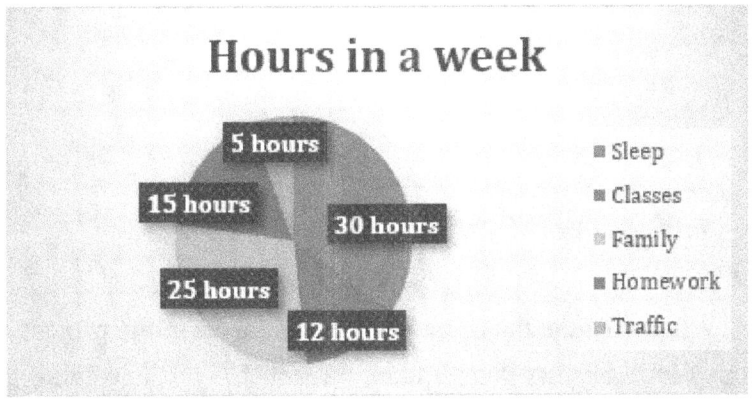

That's a nice load. Let's add in that you work a 40-hour work week because you have expenses like rent, food, and gas. With all that you have going on, your time is precious.

24 hours in a day X 5 Days a Week= 120 a week

WHAT ABOUT WEEKENDS?

It is generally recommended that students spend at least 2 hours studying for each credit hour of class. A typical three-hour class needs 6 hours of study per week-not necessarily including homework.

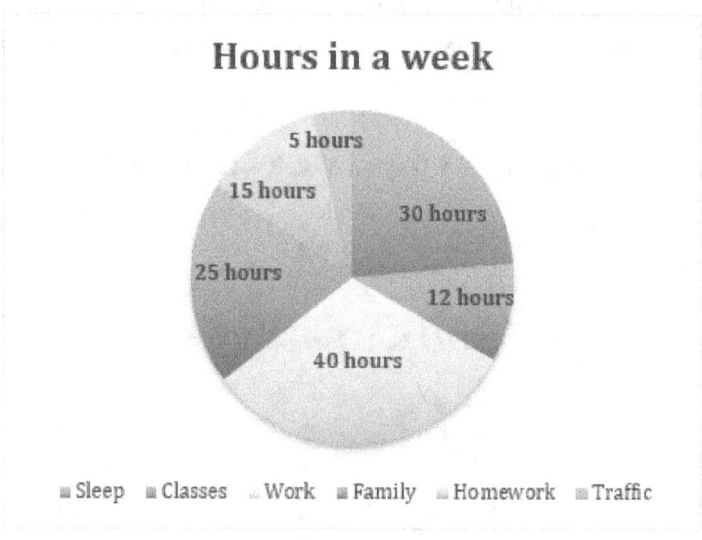

What would happen if you were assigned a group project in your World History class and an English 101 test is coming up soon, but your father suddenly became seriously ill? By the middle of the semester, your father is getting better and you believe that you can get back your focus on college but then your job announces that it plans to lay-off people. Who knows, you may be one of the people who will receive a goodbye notice. Not only does that add another level of stress in your life, but you are not mentally focused on your upcoming Chemistry test and lab project. What if then your Aunt calls and tells you that your Uncle (her husband) just passed and they are expecting you to travel from Atlanta, Georgia to Augusta, Georgia (about 3 hours away, 135 miles away).

I am guessing that I do not have to go any further with this example. Just think, if we add a child or children into the mix. This example applies to any gender, sex, or ethnicity. When life is throwing you issues, it can be a tough time to adjust. But if it's a life or death crisis, I hope that you will get counseling with a licensed therapist.

For those who are just now starting college, be aware that life cannot only throw you a curve ball, it can also throw you the whole team. When you are registering for classes, start small and do not overwhelm yourself with too many classes. You think that you can handle it, but please do not forget my advice about life. PLEASE... do not say that you need to take several classes so you can finish quickly. Like the old saying, it is not how you start the race, but it is how you finish. If you know that you have a lot going on with work and your personal life, taking a full load (another term for a full-time student) may not be the best move for you. Know and understand what you can handle. Be smart and be honest with yourself! When work feels like a headache and your personal life feels like a juggling act, guess what will suffer? If your answer is "your classes" ... Ding, Ding, Ding! You are correct!

Chapter 2

Family Educational Rights and Privacy Act (FERPA)

"You're telling me I can't see my child's information? Even though I'm the one paying for their schooling and they still live with me? This is crazy!"

The Family Educational Rights and Privacy Act (FERPA) (20 U.S.C & 1232g; 34 CFR Part 99) is a Federal law that protects the privacy of student education records. The law applies to all schools that receive funds under an applicable program of the U.S Department of Education. FERPA is the equivalent of the Health Information Portability and Accountability Act (HIPAA), for those who are in the medical field.

In other words, no one has permission to read, review, look over, discuss, or request a copy of your educational records unless you are the student, a parent with the student's permission, or anyone to whom the student gives permission with a signed FERPA document. Educational records including discussing FAFSA/financial aid information, accrediting organizations, colleges that the student is transferring to, certain officials for audit/evaluation/review purposes, medical records, showing financial aid paperwork that the student completed, immunization records, alien registration number, reading signed documentation from the student or parent, or asking teachers to see a student's grades. For the student to give a particular person permission to speak on their behalf, they must sign a FERPA/Release form from the college.

Most release forms have a section where the student can list the person(s) they would like to give permission and their relationship to the student. If you are the parent or person requesting the student's information, it is mandatory that the Financial Aid Representative or Representative from the College (Enrollment and Registration rep, Admissions Rep, or any department representative) look to see if there is a FERPA form/Release form that the student has signed and the name of the person to whom the student gives permission to look at their file.

Parents often ask, "Why do I have to get permission to look at my child's records?" or "I got to have permission to look at his records, but I am paying for his school?" or "Wait... I have to get permission to look at his records, but the FAFSA is asking for my personal information?" Those statements usually end with a curse word, a disrespectful comment, or a side eye from the parent.

Though the parents attempt to state a good rationale as to why they should know their child's (the student) information, they fail or refuse to realize that college is a business. Since college is a business, their child (student) is a client/customer and it is in the college's best interest to follow the law and keep things private unless the student gives permission to a third party. If the parent is that adamant to find out what's going on, they can simply speak with their child to gain signed permission.

Why the FERPA is beneficial:

Without a signed authorization no one can call a school or go to an office to request information that is private.

Students' information such as social security number, address, and phone number is protected.

If a Financial Aid Representative or representative from the College does not follow this rule, the student could sue the school and the school then risks losing its federal funding (Title IV). Title IV funding is extremely important because it is through this vehicle that the federal government gives money to the school. For example, Pell Grants, Subsidized Loans, Unsubsidized Loans, and Federal Work Study funds are distributed through Title IV funding.

On a personal note, I like to eat. I do not want to lose my job by breaking a law that is designed to protect the rights of students. If I do not follow the rules, none of the parents who want me to give up their child's information are not going to take me or my wife into their house to live!

Parents, if you want access to your child's information, please go with your child to the Registrar's office, fill out a FERPA form and list your name as someone who has permission to review their records. It's that simple!

Chapter 3

Knowing the Right Equipment

When you climb a mountain, do you wear bedroom slippers? Of course not! You need special boots that can help grip the mountain while you climb. For every specific activity outside, there is special training and particular attire that you must wear. In this chapter, we will explain the first steps in the college and financial aid process. In addition we will introduce you to some terminology that you should be familiar with when you visit a financial aid office.

Tour the School

"You need to see if the school is a good fit for you"

Before you begin applying to colleges and spending that $50-$100 application fee (which in most cases is non-refundable), please do research on the colleges that you are interested in attending. Unless you have $50-$100 to just give away.

> *"If you want to give away $50-$100, I will kindly instruct you to go to the back of the book and search for my email address. Once you email me and inform me that you have*

money to give away I would be delighted to give you my Cash App information."

Prior to setting up a college tour, you should begin working on your FAFSA (Free Application for Federal Student Aid) long before the term that you plan to start. We will get into more detail about the FAFSA in Chapter 4.

It's great that you reviewed the college website. Prior to touring the college go online and find out if the college has your major, what the expenses are, whether there are dorms (and costs for living there), the graduation rate, and if you and your parents/guardians are comfortable where the college is located. If you're not feeling comfortable with the information you research then that college may not be the right fit for you. But if you do find a college that checks out, then I definitely encourage you to visit the college. There's nothing like the real thing! If you don't believe me, think about this. Have you watched a fast food commercial and you see how the burger, fries, or dessert is prepared on TV? It looks marvelous and you cannot wait to get that food item. When you actually go to the restaurant and get that food item however, you might feel lied to because it was not the image that you saw from the TV.

When you are researching how much tuition costs (not just an estimate but the actual cost), also research the expected salary of the career that you are working towards. College is a business and you should treat it as such. When calculating your loan amount during your undergraduate years, it would be ridiculous to have more in debt than what you are expecting to earn once you graduate. For example, if you want to be a teacher and the annual salary is $35,000 a year but your loans amount to $80,000, then you put yourself in a major hole to try to repay your loans. Too many students are in major debt because they did not look at the total picture concerning student loans and their expected earning when they start working.

Once you have set the appointment to tour the school, or if you just decide to walk on campus to check out the college, please go to the Admissions Office so that you can understand the steps that you need to take to be officially admitted. For example, you may have to take a placement test (depending on what you made on your SATs/ACTs), and show immunization records. Most colleges require an official high school transcript and transcripts from every college you attended before. When you're visiting the admissions office, take notes and ask a lot of questions.

Know and understand the types of school you are interested in attending. Depending on the school, if you're an in-state resident or out-of-state resident, it will determine the cost of your tuition and what type of scholarship or benefits you may be eligible to receive. Please read below to learn the types of colleges and whether they are private or public institutions.

Academic Advising

Just as important as understanding your financial aid, getting advisement on your class schedule is highly vital. Your financial aid, scholarship, or simply paying out of pocket pays your tuition and other costs and getting assistance from an Academic Advisor can help you choose the right classes to take for your major. I recommend that students communicate with their Academic Advisor often, especially if you are thinking about withdrawing or changing your major. Meeting with an Academic Advisor is so necessary that many colleges will put a hold on a student's account until they have a meeting with an Academic Advisor to discuss their next steps. Your financial aid is not going to pay for a class that you have taken several times or if it's not in your major.

Creating relationships is extremely important. So, I highly recommend that you establish a relationship with your Academic Advisor. Who knows... he or she may know of a scholarship or work-study opportunity for you. Just think, it's easier to inform someone with whom they have a relationship about a possible opportunity instead of someone who they don't know at all.

Types of Colleges

It's important to know what type of college you are planning to attend because compared to state colleges private colleges are very costly. At some colleges, it is mandatory for first year students (freshmen) to stay on campus. If you plan to live on campus, you must factor in such expenses as housing, meal plans, and parking or bus/train fares.

Community College: A community college is primarily a two-year public institution for tertiary education. This higher education institution provides workforce skills and development. It also provides transferable credit to a four-year institution. Many community colleges are located near rural areas. Community Colleges are also known as junior colleges. You can receive an Associate's degree from a community college.

Historically Black Colleges and Universities (HBCU): HBCU institutions of higher education were established to give African American students equal educational opportunities as they were often not admitted to predominantly white institutions (PWI). Many of the HBCUs were established before the Civil Rights Act of 1964. There are private and public HBCUs in the United States.

Liberal Arts College: A Liberal Arts College focuses on undergraduate study in the liberal arts and sciences. These schools aim to impart a broad general knowledge and develop basic intellectual capacities, in contrast to a professional, vocational, or technical curriculum.

Private for Profit College: Known as for-profit schools. These are higher educational institutions operated by private, profit-seeking businesses.

Professional College: An institution that prepares students for careers in specific fields.

Technical College: A type of college that provides courses in practical subjects and prepares students for particular trades.

Public /State Colleges and Universities: An institution that receives public funds from the state government. Costs are typically lower than a private college or university.

College vs. University

Do you know the difference between a college and a university? Some people believe that they are the same thing. Yes, they are both tertiary institutions but there is a difference. A college is a post-secondary school in higher education that focuses on certifications, diplomas, Associates degree, or Bachelor's degree. A university is usually a larger, post-secondary school in higher education that focuses on research, undergraduate degrees, and postgraduate degrees such as Masters, Doctorate, and/or Law degrees.

In State Residency vs. Out of State Residency

Have you ever heard the statement, "Membership has its privileges?" Well you can say the same thing about your residency status. If you are an In State Resident, it simply means that you are a legal resident within that state. Out of State Residency is the opposite: you are not a legal resident of the state. This is critical to know because of the cost of tuition. Out of state residency causes the cost of tuition to almost double compared to tuition for an In State Resident. I have personally seen students who had to drop out of college because they couldn't afford the Out of State Residency rate. They will have to wait for a year to be recognized as a legal resident of the state so they could receive the lower tuition rate.

Besides the cost of tuition, another factor that is beneficial to In-State Residency students is the grants and scholarships that the state will award to the legal resident. For example, one criteria of the HOPE Scholarship and Zell Miller Scholarship in the state of Georgia is that you must be a legal resident of the state.

As stated earlier, the cost of tuition for an Out of State Resident is much higher compared to the cost of an In-State resident. Depending on where you live within the state, there are certain colleges and areas from another state that will recognize you as an In-State resident based on the fact that you are in a neighboring state. This is called Reciprocity.

If you have any issues with your residency status, I advise you to speak with your college's Admissions Office.

Public vs. Private

When researching colleges, another factor to be considered is the tuition cost of attending a public college/university or private college/university. A public college/university is funded by the state government and gets Title IV funding like the Pell Grant and Subsidized as well as Unsubsidized loans. Funding from the state government helps with the cost of attendance by lowering tuition fees for their students. Public colleges and universities receive benefits from the state such as state scholarships (e.g.: HOPE Scholarship and Zell Miller Scholarship in Georgia).

Private colleges and universities also receive Title IV funding; however, much of their funding is by fundraising for their endowment and they are not operated by the government. With Title IV funding, the private college/university is subject to government regulations. Private colleges and universities are more expensive because they depend on student's tuition and fee payments to cover operating expenses.

Academic Award Year Calendar

Traditionally, the Academic Year does not follow the Calendar year but rather runs from July 1 – June 30. This is an important distinction as it affects when applications are due and when funds are disbursed.

Example of an Academic Semester Year Calendar

Classes Begin	Classes End
(Fall 2021) August 23, 2021	December 6, 2021
(Spring 2022) January 10, 2022	April 25, 2022
(Summer 2022) June 6, 2022,	July 25, 2022

Also of interest is whether the school is on a Quarter/Module System or on a Semester System. Unlike the

15-16 weeks in a semester, the Module or Quarter System is normally three months (summer schedules are usually shorter for both). Unlike the semesters, the Quarter System could cross two award years. To illustrate, if you start school on June 7, 2021 and your Module or Quarter System ends on July 30, 2021, then you started in the 2020-2021-award year and you crossed into the 2021-2122-award year.

Example of the Module or Quarter System Academic Year

Classes Begin	Classes End
(1st Quarter) August 23, 2021	October 19, 2021
(2nd Quarter) October 25, 2021	December 16, 2021
(3rd Quarter) January 18, 2022	February 15, 2022
(4th Quarter) March 28, 2022	May 17, 2022
(Summer 2022) June 13, 2022	July 22, 2022

Frequently asked Questions

I will often have long discussions with students and parents in my office about financial aid and I give them advice on what to do and not to do in college. Many of the students that I work with are the first in their family to go to college. Besides being excited to attend college, many don't understand or realize the questions that they should be asking staff, the Admission Representatives, or those who host New Student Orientations. Please take note of a suggested list of questions below.

1. What documents do I need to get admitted to college?
2. Did you receive my official transcripts?
3. What makes this college different than any colleges in the area?
4. Does this college have a scholarship department? Is so, where is it located?
5. What is the graduation rate for the college?
6. Since I live in another state, is it possible for me to receive in-state tuition?
7. For those intending to stay in campus housing or the dorm, will they be able to know or meet their roommate ahead of time?
8. How much is housing or the dorm? Is a meal plan included?
9. Could a student get an escort to their car or dorm at night?
10. Where is the campus police department and where is the closest city/county police office?
11. Besides work-study, can a student get a job on campus?
12. Is the college an open campus?
13. If there were an emergency that is happening at the college, how would the students be contacted?

14. Does this college have a COVID protocol?
15. Would I have to show proof of my COVID immunization?
16. What if I am not vaccinated?
17. If I want to change my major, to which department would I go?
18. To which office should I go to complete a FERPA form to give permission to a 3rd party to discuss my account?
19. Does this college have a job placement office?
20. How is the relationship with the college and the community?
21. Does the college help students to receive co-op or internship opportunities?
22. Where is the office for the counselor or therapist on campus?
23. Where can students get a parking pass?
24. Is there a bus line by the college?
25. How far is the airport from the college?
26. Can students get a discount on bus or transit tickets?
27. As a freshman, am I allowed to drive my vehicle for the first year?
28. Where is the learning and tutoring center on campus?
29. Where is the library and what are the opening hours?

30. Where can a student learn about the different organizations or clubs on campus? Will there be a club fair?

31. Is there a special area where students can go to protest?

32. Could students create their own organizations on campus?

33. Are students allowed to carry a gun on campus?

34. How can a student participate in the Study Abroad program?

35. Do the college accept payment through flywire?

36. Does the college provide insurance or do we need to get our own?

37. Where is the hospital or Urgent Care in the area?

38. What banks or credit unions are in the area?

39. Does the college pay for off campus housing?

40. Is there a military/VA center on campus?

41. When is the deadline to pay all tuition and fees?

42. What forms of payment does the Cashier/Bursar Office accepts?

Chapter 4

Preparing for the Mountain of Financial Aid

"How can I receive financial aid?"

Many families do not have the means to pay out of pocket for college, so they rely heavily on the FAFSA. As a Financial Aid Representative, it's my job to educate students on what aid we (the university and FAFSA) are able to offer and what you may qualify for. When a student or family member walks into my office, I never want them to feel embarrassed that they do not know anything about financial aid or college in general. I'm a firm believer that you have to start somewhere! Today, we still have many students who are the first ones in their family to attend college. The first key point in order to receive financial aid from the federal government, a student must declare a major.

FAFSA

The most important step to receive financial aid from the federal government is to submit the for Free Application for Federal Student Aid (FAFSA). The FAFSA is filled with questions that will determine how much financial aid a student may be eligible for. There will be questions that pertain to your current address, the student's family situation, student's educational background, prospective colleges, the spouse finances, tax-filing status, and many other pertinent questions. If you are a Dependent Student, you will have questions that will pertain to your parents. You can go online to www.studentaid.gov to complete the FAFSA.

> *WWW.STUDENTAID.GOV is the official FAFSA Website. There are other websites that will charge you a fee. Applying to the FAFSA is "FREE."*

Once you submit your request for financial aid, your FAFSA will be examined to make sure you are the correct person who is filing a FAFSA and to make sure that all data matches. Typically it takes between three to five business days before an ISIR (record of the FAFSA) comes to the school. Once the school receives the ISIR, a financial aid representative will review the results of your FAFSA for approval or rejection. Common reasons why a student's FAFSA is rejected are: information is missing, citizenship concerns, student is in default, or data that does not match. You may go into a financial aid office so the financial aid representative can tell you what information is missing. Students can also find out what they are missing through their student portal and/or an email or letter sent by the financial aid office.

If you're planning to attend school around this time.	When you can submit your FAFSA	Tax Information to Use	FAFSA
July 1, 2021- June 30, 2022	October 1, 2020- June 30, 2021	2019	2021-2022
July 1, 2022- June 30, 2023	October 1, 2021- June 30, 2022	2020	2022-2023
July 1, 2023- June 30, 2024	October 1, 2022- June 30, 2023	2021	2023-2024
July 1, 2024- June 30, 2025	October 1, 2023- June 30, 2024	2022	2024-2025

Prior Prior Year

Prior Prior Year means that you may submit your tax returns from two years ago, instead of turning in your tax information from the previous year. This change became effective in October 2016.

Source: *National Association of Student Financial Aid Administrators* *https://www.nasfaa.org/ppyresources*

Tell the Truth

When completing your FAFSA, please make sure that all the information is accurate and correct. Please DO NOT FALSIFY any information on your FAFSA. The FAFSA is a legal, government document. If it is discovered that you falsified information on your FAFSA, you will get hit with a penalty, which could be a fine or potential jail time.

How to Complete the FAFSA

Before starting the FAFSA, please make sure you have all the necessary documents with you.

> A. **Tax Return Papers:** If you have filed taxes, you will need to have a copy of your 1040, 1040A, or 1040EZ. The FAFSA does have an option called the Data Retrieval Tool that allows you to upload your tax information from the IRS to the FAFSA; however, it's great to have this information as a backup in case the system starts acting up. If you're not able to use the Data Retrieval Tool, you can review FAFSA. On the FAFSA, there is a section where you can find the answer to specific question questions.
>
> **Example:** What was your (and spouse's) adjusted gross income for 2019? Adjusted gross income is on IRS Form 1040-line 37; 1040A- line 21; or 1040EZ-line 4.
>
> - When it comes to your Tax Return Papers, please remember that students/parents will report their tax information from two years earlier. For example, on the 2021-2022 FAFSA, you will report your 2019 Tax Return

information. For the 2022-2023, you will report your 2020 Tax Return information.

- The IRS Data Retrieval Tool should make it easy to upload information from your tax information onto your FAFSA. If you were able to use the Data Retrieval process, you would not need your tax return papers; however, if the Data Retrieval Tool were not working, then you would manually put in the tax information from your tax returns. Depending on which tax return you file, the FAFSA will give you the number(s) and mathematical information to place on the FAFSA.

B. **Alien Registration Number:** If you are not a US Citizen, you would be required to enter this information.

C. **FSA_ID**: Student's username and password login information that can be used to e-sign your FAFSA. If the student is a dependent student, their parent would need to create their own FSA ID. The FSA ID verifies your identity by matching your legal name, social security number, and date of birth. Be sure to keep this information safe. It is important to use an email address that the student/parent can always access. Connecting the FSA ID to a school or work email is not advised.

- When it comes to your passwords, please, please, please write it down and keep it in a place that you can remember. If you lose your password, you will need to contact the actual FAFSA customer service line so they can help you to reset your FSA ID. We all know that when you call the federal government, the wait time can be extremely long so keep track of you FSA ID and password so you won't have to endure such a wait. If you are a parent, you would need to create an FSA ID. You can use the same FSA ID for your child and yourself if you are in school.

D. **Records of untaxed income:** Information that includes child support, interest income, and veterans' non-educational benefits.

E. **Social Security Number:** Your social security number is needed to verify that you are the correct person.

F. **Driver's License:** If you have a valid driver's license, the FAFSA will ask if you would like to provide this number.

In my experience, many school counselors assist students in completing the FAFSA, which is really good. BUT... when it's time to renew their FAFSA, several students and their parents do not know what to do and need help. A financial aid representative is there to help, but it's very empowering if a student or parent knows and understands how to fill out documentation himself or herself. Instead of going to the college, they can simply fill out the FAFSA at home. To my school counselor, don't just teach, but please make sure the student fully understands the documentation.

If you have a Bachelor's Degree from the United States or any other country, you will not be eligible to receive the Pell Grant. The Pell Grant is for undergraduate students seeking an Associates Degree, Bachelor's Degree or Certificate.

Tell the TRUTH! DO NOT LIE on your FAFSA. It's one thing to simply make a mistake but it is a whole different ball of wax to lie to try to get additional financial aid. The FAFSA is a federal document, if you lie and get caught you will be penalized.

I had a student who was frustrated because he owed money to the college. He wanted to know why and why he was withdrawn from his classes. While reviewing his financial aid, he stated on his FAFSA application that he did not have a Bachelor's Degree but in fact he did. He was awarded a Pell Grant but after the discovery, his Pell Grant was rescinded which meant that the college took away his Pell Grant and he had to pay back the funds from the Pell Grant that he used to pay his tuition.

Once the college has your FAFSA, a financial aid counselor will review your status and discuss it with you. Trust me, a financial aid counselor wants your financial aid to be right and for the process to go smoothly. College is a business. If we don't have customers (students), then the doors cannot be open. Besides receiving financial aid money for college, the ultimate goal is to receive the Pell Grant, which is the free money that does not have to be repaid. Will all students be eligible for the Pell Grant? The answer is No. It is always good to apply for the FAFSA because there are other state and institutional grant options that require the FAFSA to be completed, but do not require a student to be eligible for the Pell Grant.

If your financial aid counselor gives you advice, please follow it. If you do not understand, please let the financial aid counselor know or ask to speak with a manager. We want you to leave our offices fully understanding what's going on with your account.

Too many times students listen to their peers, professors, or others who do not know what's going on with their accounts. The friend who is giving you advice may have a full scholarship, and you have loans only. When it comes to your financial aid, please speak to the financial aid counselors for the best information and advice.

Chapter 5

Dependent vs. Independent

"I'm 21 years old, with my own place, my own car, and I pay my own bills, and I still have to use my parent information?"

One of the many topics of discussion that I have with students is the difference between a dependent student and an independent student. I have had a 21-year-old student come into my office, upset, and telling me that she is an independent student. I informed her that she does not meet the criteria of an independent student.

"I pay my own bills, I got my own place, and I don't ask my parents for anything!"

This is usually the response that I receive from students. Seeing the frustration in their faces, with a soft tone, I gently inform them that I do not make the rules; I just inform them what the rules are and help them comply.

You are considered a dependent student when we need your parent(s) information to complete the FAFSA. To be recognized as an independent student, you must comply with one of the following criteria:

- Student is 24 years old or older.
- Student's parents are deceased/last living parent dies, student is in foster care, or a ward of the court.
- Student is currently serving in "active duty" in the armed forces. It cannot be for training or reserves.
- Student is married or separated from spouse.
- The student and their parent have been separated and the U.S Immigration Service grants their status as a refugee.
- Student is homeless or at risk of being homeless.
- Student is an emancipated child as determined by a court judge.

In some situations, the college may need to do a Professional Judgment to upgrade a student's independent status. A Professional Judgment gives special authority to a financial aid administrator (typically a manager) to make adjustments to the data from the FAFSA by overriding a student's dependent status. Over the years, there have been many different situations and scenarios that have made the student financial service counselors review and re-examine the independence status.

Chapter 6

FAFSA Aftermath

"I did my FAFSA last week, so, what's my next step?"

It typically takes 3-5 business days until the college receives any information about your FAFSA. The college will receive an ISIR (processed information/report from the completed FAFSA). Once the college receives the ISIR report, one of three things will occur: 1) your FAFSA could get rejected, 2) selected for verification, or 3) financial aid is ready to be processed.

Once a student submit the FAFSA, the student should receive a Student Aid Report (SAR). If you provided an email address on your FAFSA, the SAR should come to you electronically within 3-5 business days. If a student mails in their FAFSA, they will receive a PDF version in the mail within a couple of weeks. The SAR is important because a student and parent want to make sure that the information is correct because the data that is listed will be used to determine your financial aid award.

FAFSA has been rejected

If your FAFSA was rejected, a financial aid representative could see the reason why via the ISIR. Below are just some of the reasons:

A. **Missing Parent(s) Information:** There could be some missing information that we need to review the file. If you are a Dependent Student, you will need parent(s) information. We will need one of your parent's signatures (FSA ID), social security number, asset information, marital status, address, and date of birth.

B. **Social Security Numbers do not match**: When a FAFSA is submitted, the data that you provided will be reviewed by the Social Security Administration database. If the name does not match the social security number, it will be flagged in the system and rejected.

C. **Gross and Net Amount data is not correct**: Your gross amount and net amount cannot be the same. The reason why is because the "gross amount" is what you have earned in a particular year (before taxes) and the "net amount" is what you take home (minus taxes and other deductions) from your paycheck. Ex: You cannot say that you made $30,000 in 2019 and then say that you take home $30,000 in 2019.

D. **Default**: If you have a federal direct loan from a college or university and failed to make a payment or arrangement and that loan is now 270 days past due. The federal government will not allow you to receive financial aid because you owe money on a loan. To get back in good standing, the student would have to either pay off their loans in full or get into a loan rehabilitation or loan consolidation program. If the student has any inquiries or comments about their loans, they would need to call the Department of Education. This is not something that a school's financial aid counselor would be able to resolve.

E. **No FSA signature**: Once you finish with your FAFSA, the student or one parent (if student is a Dependent student) must e-sign the FAFSA with your FSA ID.

F. **Proof of Citizenship:** If you are not from the United States, you may be asked to show proof of citizenship. The purpose of showing your proof of citizenship is to show if your Visa is expired or that you are an eligible non-citizen. Once proof of citizenship is received, the information will be reviewed through the Homeland Security database.

Selected You for Verification

Once the school receives your ISIR, it may need additional information to either confirm information that you stated or to clarify the information that you provided. The school needs these additional documents to further process your file. Examples of why you may be selected for verification.

A. **Marital Status:** On your FAFSA, you stated that you are married, but on your taxes, it states that you are the Head of the Household. This would lead to verification due to the marital status. If you are married, you must file Married filing Jointly or Married filing Separately. Head of Households filings are for the one parent that has a child or children that they are claiming (their dependents). Filing Single would be only if you are claiming yourself. If you are separated or divorced, you can claim Head of Household status but in some cases, you must provide proof of divorce or separation.

If you were married in the year that we are asking for on the FASFA, and now you are separated or divorced, the school may ask you to fill out a form or bring proof of your separation. The financial aid department should be able to inform you of the documents needed as proof. An example of a document that proves that you are divorced is a divorce decree. Once you provide the necessary document(s), the financial aid department moves ahead with the process.

B. **Making Changes**: The college/university receives your FAFSA and awarded you financial aid; however, you went back onto your FAFSA to make corrections and sent it off to the school. This would be a red flag to the college because a student may manipulate the system to see if they could receive additional financial aid money. The school will typically ask for documents such as tax returns or tax transcripts from the IRS, wage and income transcript from the IRS, tax returns, or proof of dependents.

C. **Social Security Number doesn't match:** If your social security number doesn't match the Social Security Administration records, the school will request either your birth certificate, driver's license, or a signed social security card.

D. **Selective Service:** By law, all 18 year-old males must register with the selective service within 30 days of their birthday. If you did not register for the selective service, then you would not be eligible for any financial aid. After you turn 26 years old, it will be too late for a male to register. If you are over the age of 26 years old, you must provide a valid reason to why you did not register for the selective service. For example, if you moved into this country after you turn 26 years old, you must show proof of when you entered this country. A valid document of proof would be your Passport when you entered into this country. A male can go online and register for selective service by going onto www.sss.gov. Students can also be registered as part of completing the FAFSA.

Often students have asked me, "Why am I selected for Verification?" or "Why are you guys picking on me?" My response, "we want to make sure that we have the correct information and we are not trying to pick on you." We need to make sure we have the correct paperwork and supporting documents.

Financial Aid is ready to be processed

If your FAFSA has not been selected for verification or if a student who was selected for verification has turned in all the requested documents, the next step would be for the student's financial aid to be processed. The financial aid processor will review and examine the data from the FAFSA and verification document(s) for any discrepancies. If there is an issue, the student will be informed. A financial aid counselor will try to communicate with the student by their college, student email address. If there's no issue, the financial aid will be processed and the student will be awarded financial aid. If the student is not officially admitted, we cannot award the student their financial aid; however, the file can be reviewed.

The Financial Aid Department is not responsible for the Cost of Tuition for the College. If you are an Out of State-Student/Non-Resident, your tuition would cost more than an In-State Student. If a student wants to discuss their residency, the student should speak to the Admissions Office.

Transient Student/Consortium Agreement

A student can attend two colleges or universities at the same time; however, financial aid will be disbursed at only one school.

How is this possible?

One way that it is possible is if the student just pays out of pocket at the other college or university (host school) that they hope to attend while using financial aid at their home school. The other way is by becoming a transient student and having the colleges and universities sign a consortium agreement.

A transient student is a student who is enrolled in one college or university (home school/primary school) and is taking courses on a temporary basis at another college or university (host school) with the goal of transferring the credits that they are taking at their host school back to their home school. Before a student becomes a transient student, it's a good idea to discuss their courses with an academic advisor and review which courses will transfer?

A consortium agreement is an agreement or contract between two colleges/universities (home school and host school) that acknowledges your registration at both schools for financial aid and credit purposes. Only your home school can administer your financial aid from Title IV and state awards.

Although you are a transient student and your consortium agreement was approved, I encourage you to speak with the financial aid department to ask how the college handles transient students. Why? Because college is a business. For some schools, once you become a transient student and your financial aid will be coming from your home school, the host school will be looking for a payment for insurance purpose for the student and school. No, I'm not talking about life insurance or health insurance. I am speaking about making sure that time and money are not wasted. Look at it this way, you began classes at your host school believing that you had enough financial aid to cover your school. Weeks go by in the semester and then you receive a notification from the Student Accounts/Bursar office that you have a balance on your account. You are thinking that you should be good in regards to your financial aid. Well, in reality you used up your eligibility at your home school. Now, you are in a dilemma to try to pay for your classes. You don't have the money and will be dropped from your classes and will owe a balance.

If a student does have financial aid at their home school, once tuition has been paid for at their home school, and if the student is eligible; then they can receive a refund for the class or classes that they paid for at their host school.

College is a business. Just as important as a student receiving an education, a college or university must receive funding to operate.

Chapter 7

Estimated Family Contribution (EFC)

"What determines how much financial aid I can receive?"

Once you complete your FAFSA, it normally takes 3-5 business days to process your information and send it to your selected school in the form of an ISIR. Your FAFSA may give you an estimate; however, once it comes to the school, the processors will review your financial aid eligibility to determine how much Pell Grant and loans a student is eligible for - especially if that student attended another university/college during that same semester-award year.

The Estimated Family Contribution (EFC) is a major factor in determining how much financial aid you will receive. The EFC is based on information from the student and parent (if student is a dependent student) stated on the FAFSA. This information would include: household size, income, assets, whether you received free or reduced price school lunches, if you are a dislocated worker, the number of people in your household and how many of those are attending college. The EFC uses a formula that determines the eligibility on specific types of financial aid. For example, Pell Grants, Loans, Federal Supplemental Educational Opportunity Grants (FSEOG) and

Work Study. When it comes to your Pell Grant, your EFC will determine how much grant money you may receive. Once you receive your Pell Grant, it will adjust for the number of credit hours you are taking in school.

Knowing your EFC is important because it determines if you are eligible for the full amount of Pell Grant, a partial amount, or if you qualify at all. To receive the full Pell Grant, your EFC must be 0.

If you have used the Pell Grant at a previous college and are attempting to return to school and receive financial aid, it is important to know how much Pell funding you have remaining. That's right - there's no such thing as a never-ending Pell Grant amount. The lifetime limit of Pell Grant is 600% that equates to 6 years. In other words, the Pell Grant limit is contingent on years, not dollar amount. If you are taking 12 credit hours or more (full time student), each year as a full time student represents 100% with 600% the max. Depending on a student's Pell Grant amount (credit hours they are taking), can affect his or her percentage in receiving the Pell Gant.

When students want to know how much Pell Grant they can receive, a financial aid counselor will first look at the EFC. Once we get that information, we follow the spreadsheet to see their maximum amount available for this award term. Depending on how many credit hours a student is taking we can then estimate the amount of Pell Grant a student may receive.

Students who are close to their overall Pell Grant limit may receive a lesser amount, or no funding.

Understanding the EFC

Parents and students often ask: "Is there a certain amount of credit hours that I need to take to get my financial aid?" The answer is yes; however, it depends primarily on your EFC. If you were awarded loans, you would need to be at least a half-time student (6 credit hours). When it comes to your Pell Grant, it will adjust, depending on how many credit hours you take. Let us review The Pell Chart.

Note: *Whether and how much Pell Grant you receive is affected by: whether or not you are making Satisfactory Academic Progress (SAP); whether you are approaching the Maximum Time Frame; PACE Ratio; GPA: whether you are in default, and the amount of Pell Grant that you have remaining (lifetime).*

0 EFC Example

EFC	12 Credit Hours or More	9-11 Credit Hours	6-8 Credit Hours	1-5 Credit Hours
0	6495= 3248/3247	4871= 2346/2435	3248= 1624/1624	1624= 812/812

In this first box, you have EFC which stands for Estimated Family Contribution. Your EFC is based on the student (if dependent student, their parents) tax information. Underneath the EFC box will be numbers. 0 will always be the first number on top. 0 represents the full Pell Grant amount that you are eligible to receive. The closer you are to 0, the more Pell Grant eligibility that you will receive.

The Pell Grant will adjust to how many credit hours that you are taking. If you are taking 12 credit hours or more, there's a set amount., 9-11 credit hours, there's a set amount, 6-8 credit hours, there's a set amount, and finally 1-5 credit hours is a set amount. For example, if you are taking 7 credit hours, you are not going to get the same Pell Grant amount as if you are taking 12 credit hours. Understanding the EFC, you will know how much your Pell Grant amount is for the year. For example, if your EFC is 0, you can look for the number in the box, scroll over to the 12 Credit Hours or More (6495) to see how much you are awarded.

The amount of the Pell Grant change from year to year and that the current figures are based on the 2021-2022 award year.

The next box is 12 Credit Hours or More. If you are taking 12 Credit hours or More, it means that you are a full time student. Under the 12 Credit Hours or More box is 6495=3248/3247. The first number (6495) represents Pell Grant overall eligibility that is $6495. The 3248/3247 combination represents half of the $6495. If you take 12 credit hours in the

Fall 2021, you will be awarded $3248. In that same award year, if you take 12 credit hours in the Spring 2022, you will receive $3247.

What if a student decides to go to school in the Spring 2022 and Summer 2022 and not in the Fall 2021, would the student still receive financial aid? The answer is yes. When a student is awarded, it goes for the entire award year. Just as we did in the example above, if a student is enrolled in 12 credit hours in the Spring 2022 and 12 credit hours in the Summer 2022, the student will still receive $3248 in the Spring 2022 and $3247 in the Summer 2022. The same way how we broke down the 12 Credit Hours and More, you can use the same formula for 9-11 credit hours, 6-8 credit hours, and 1-5 credit hours.

Scenario 1: Jamie is taking 7 credit hours in the Fall 2021 and 6 credit hours in the Spring 2022. How much Pell Grant should she receive? You can review the Pell Chart box and see the 6-8 credit hours.

Answer: *Fall 2021- $1624   Spring 2022-$1624*

Scenario 2: Mary would like to take 12 credit hours in the Fall 2021 and 7 credit hours in the Spring 2022. How much financial aid award should she receive? Let's review the data. Reviewing the box, if you have a 0 EFC, the overall amount of Pell Grant that you are awarded for this 2021-2022 award year is $6,495. If you take 12 credit hours for the Fall 2021, you will be awarded $3248. For the Spring 2022, let's look at the 6-8 credit hours box. The student would be awarded $1624.

Bonus: With the same example, if a student wants to go to school in the summer, how much Pell Grant money does he or she has remaining?

$6495- overall award amount

-$3248- Fall 2021 (12 credit hours)

$3247

-$1624- Spring 2022 (6 credit hours)

$1623 available for the summer

Reviewing what you have available and the Pell Chart, you can see that you have up to 8 credit hours that your Pell Grant will pay for your tuition.

301-400 EFC Example

If your EFC were not 0, how would someone know their Pell Grant amount? Just as the example above with the 0 EFC, we can do the same thing with any number. Below is a chart that if your EFC was a number between 301-400, we can see the amount of Pell Grant funding that you will be eligible to receive based on the number of credit hours taken. Just remember, the closer you are to an EFC of 0, the more money you can receive. Your EFC is based off of your tax and household information for a certain year. The same concept as a 0 EFC is used to determine how much Pell Grant eligibility that a student has.

EFC	12 Credit Hours or More	9-11 Credit Hours	6-8 Credit Hours	1-5 Credit Hours
301-400	6145= 3073/3072	4609= 2305/2304	3073= 1537/1536	1536= 768/768

Scenario 3: Kenneth has an EFC of 370. He would like to take 11 credit hours for the Spring 2022 term. How much Pell Grant would he be eligible to receive?

>**Answer:** *Once you see the 301-400 and realize that 370 falls in between 301-400, you scroll across the 9-11 credit hours data. $2305 is the amount of Pell Grant that the student would be eligible to obtain.*

Scenario 4: Patsy has an EFC of 303. She is looking to take 4 credit hours in the Fall 2021 and 9 credit hours in the Spring 2022. How much Pell Grant should she expect in the Fall 2021 and Spring 2022? Would she have enough for Summer 2022?

>**Answer:** *Looking over to the 1-5 credit hours, Patsy should be eligible to receive $768 in the Fall 2021. Since she plans to take 9 credit hours in the Spring 2022, she should be eligible to receive $2305.*

$6145 (overall Pell Grant eligibility with an EFC of 303)

-$768 (Fall 2021 Pell Grant- 4 credit hours)

$5377

-$2305 (Spring 2022 Pell Grant- 9 credit hours)

$3072 **Patsy is eligible to take up to 12 credit hours (full time for the Summer 2022)**

If a student takes 12 credit hours or more (full time) in the fall semester and 12 credit hours or more (full time) in the spring semester and if their EFC is 0, a student can be eligible to receive additional Pell Grant for the summer semester if the student is taking a minimum of 6 credit hours. This is only for the Pell Grant, not for any loans.

Chapter 8

Loans

"I quit my job so I can start school fulltime. I need these loans so I can survive. So, can you tell me how can I get these loans?"

Loans are not an easy subject to discuss. Loans can be as complicated as someone wanting to climb a mountain barefooted in the rain. Many people were never taught finance, credit, and budgeting, so when it comes to discussing loans, all they know is that you have to pay the money back. Never fully reading the master promissory note, they never know who is a lender, what happens when a person can't pay back what they borrowed, or why interest rates are important?

I was inspired to write this by a few students who would come into my office, frustrated and ticked off, or needing a loan for personal reasons. Sometimes they would have a million questions about getting a loan and how loans work. Others would say that they regret getting a loan because it's tough for them to make payments. On a personal level, I wanted to educate you on how loans work. So, before I discuss the different types of college loans let me first break down loans in general.

I have had several students and parents tell me that they do not want a loan because loans are the devil. I wonder why they say that. Is it because they would have to pay back what the spent? I was told that in certain cultures it's against their religion. I'm not going to say that loans are the devil because unless we have someone who is able to assist us financially, we may all need loans to help us out whether it's to pay college tuition or money to start a business. The goal is to know how much you are taking out and at what interest rate. Take out only as much as you need and don't allow anyone to pressure you to take out a loan if you do not feel comfortable in doing so.

What are loans?

Loans are monies borrowed from a lender with the expectation that the funds must be paid back to the lender with interest.

The lender is a person, bank, or federally regulated government agency that has money to lend. Since this is a business, the goal is to make money from lending you (the student) money by charging you interest.

Once you receive a loan, there is an origination fee that will be subtracted from your loan. An origination fee is an upfront cost of processing a new loan application and establishing it. An origination fee is usually a set amount, depending on what type of loan you are receiving. For a student loan, the percentage of an origination fee varies from 0.5%-1%. In other words, if you borrowed $1,000, the origination fee maybe $10. Instead of you receiving the full $1,000 that you requested, you will only receive $990. YES... you will have to repay $1,000 plus the interest on the loan.

To receive any federal student loan(s), a student must be a halftime student (taking a minimum of 6 credit hours) and not to be in default. Once a student accepts the loan, the student must complete a Master Promissory Note (MPN) and entrance counseling. A master promissory note is a legal contract between the lender (the person or group that issues the funds) and the borrower (the student) that states that you are accepting the loan and the responsibilities that are attached to it and that you intend to pay back the loan plus the interest and any fees.

Students can go onto the *studentaid.gov* website to complete the entrance counseling and master promissory note (MPN) if they are seeking to obtain a federal student loan. If you are graduating, currently enrolled below half-time, or have stopped attending classes, you need to complete an exit counseling. If you are not looking to receive a federal student loan, you do not have to complete an entrance counseling and master promissory note. To make it easier for you, you can cancel your federal student loan. *Studentaid.gov* is a federal government website. Once you complete the entrance counseling, master promissory note, and exit counseling, an email will be sent to you confirming that you have completed each part.

To illustrate, the lender is expecting that the borrower will pay the interest that is attached to the loan and pay the loan on time. If not, there will be late penalties added on to the debt. A master promissory note will normally ask for three references. The reason they ask for references is that if they cannot get in contact with the borrower, they will contact one of their references to inform them that they have an outstanding balance and they need to contact the lender to have the situation resolved.

Entrance Counseling is an activity that educates the borrower (student) on budgeting and finance. The entrance counseling helps the student by counseling them and helping them to understand and to think about their own personal finance and the responsibility they will take on by accepting the loan.

Another counseling you should be aware of is exit counseling. Exit counseling occurs when you are finished with school or you go below the halftime status. The purpose of the exit counseling is to educate a student on repayment options and to remind the student that they have a loan that they must pay back.

Scenario

We have reviewed various terms common misunderstandings and the importance of understanding what you are getting into. I hope you understand everything so far. To give you an even better understanding let's look at some "what if" situations in the scenarios below.

Scenario 1: Daniel Jones' financial aid was processed and he was offered a $1,750 student loan for college. Since he was a halftime student (taking at least the minimum of 6 credit hours, but less than the full-time 12 hours), he decided to accept the loan. Before he could receive the loan, his financial aid advisor informed him that he must go on line to www.studentaid.gov to complete an entrance counseling and sign the master promissory note. After doing this, Daniel was informed that the origination fee for his loan was 1%.

> **$1,750 (subsidized loan) X .01% (percentage of origination fee) = $17.50 origination fee**
>
> **$1,750 (subsidized loan) - $17.50 (origination fee) = $1732.50 (the actual loan amount you will receive)**
>
> **Yes, he will have to pay for $1,750 and not just the $1,732.50 that he actually received.**

Scenario 2: Gina needed another loan to help her with the remaining balance. She decided to get an unsubsidized loan for $1,000. When she looked over her account, she only saw $990. She was shocked and confused. Gina asked one of the financial aid counselors to explain to her why she didn't receive the full $1,000.

> **$1,000 (unsubsidized loan) X .01% (percentage of the origination loan) =$10.00**
>
> **$1,000 (unsubsidized loan) - $10.00= $990.00**

The student will have to pay the $1,000 plus interest (because it is an unsubsidized loan).

Types of Loans

It is important to remember that ALL LOANS MUST BE REPAID! Whether you pay interest from the beginning of the loan or after you have finished school, the money from loans has to be paid back. Let me share with you the three main types of student loans: private loans such as from a bank or commercial financial institution; subsidized federal loans and unsubsidized federal loans. Grants, such as the PELL Grant are not loans but free money that does not have to be repaid. When your financial aid application has been processed, many people only think about the Pell Grant, however you may also be offered loans – which you do not have to accept. Let's take a moment to discuss the differences between a subsidized loan and unsubsidized loan.

Subsidized Loan: This is the loan where the government pays the interest while you are in school. In other words, you only pay what you borrowed. If you have to choose between loans, this would be the best option.

Unsubsidized Loan: This is the loan where the student is responsible for the interest. The interest will start once the loan has been issued.

Parent Loan for Undergraduate Students (PLUS Loan): This is the only federal student loan that your parent can take on the loan payment. The PLUS loans are for dependent undergraduate students and graduate/professional students. How does the PLUS loan work? The student's parent would need to go onto www.studentaid.gov to complete the application for the PLUS loan, complete an entrance counseling, and review information on the master promissory note. Once they are registered, their credit will be checked. If the parent's credit is approved, the loan will be issued and the parent will be responsible for the payments. If the parent's credit is denied, the student would receive an offer of an additional $2,500 of unsubsidized loans. While it might sound great to receive extra money, don't forget that an unsubsidized loan where the student is responsible for the interest from Day One. That means that the student will be responsible for paying back even more money than originally borrowed.

If a student chooses to take a loan, it is the student's responsibility to pay it off, unless you are a parent whose been approved for the PLUS loan. With the PLUS loan the parents are responsible for repaying the loan. I have actually had students to say "Do I have to pay the loan back?" or "Why do I have to pay the loan back?" or "I didn't know I had a loan! or even "You know that I couldn't pay that money back, that's you guys loss!" If you have any questions regarding your financial aid, I highly recommend you speak with a financial aid counselor before your financial aid is disbursed.

Students, please understand that you must repay your loans. If you do not, you will be in default, which means you will not be eligible for any financial aid and the federal government may garnish your salary and take away your income tax refunds.

6-Month Grace Period

When a student has graduated, leaves school, or drops below half-time status, you will be given a 6-month grace period before repayment is required. This means that within six months, you do not have to start making any payments on your loans for those first six months. After that you will receive a notification from your lender that repayment is due and information about your loan repayment options. A student can begin making payments on their loans while they are in school, if they choose too. They will need to communicate with a lender.

In-School Deferment

If you have graduated from a college or university, using federal student loans, or have attended a college from which you did not graduate using federal student loans, and plan on enrolling another college, I strongly advise you to apply for an In-School Deferment. An In-School Deferment will postpone your previous loan(s) so you don't have to pay on them until you are finished with school. Go to the Registrar's office at your school and have them complete the In-School Deferment form. This is necessary because your lender needs to have proof that you are enrolled in classes at a college. The Registrar will communicate to the lender that you are in school. Deferring your loan payment does not necessarily mean interest is not still accruing.

DEFAULT

If you do not make a payment for 270 days, then you will be considered in default –you OWE the federal government money and have failed to meet the obligation of paying on a loan. Once you are in default, you cannot receive any type of financial aid until your debt has been paid or a payment plan has been approved. If you are in default it is difficult to get employment in certain jobs. Just think about this... when you apply for a job, does it ask the question "Do you owe the federal government?" Well... student loans are monies from the federal government. As mentioned earlier, not paying on your loan(s) can negatively impact your credit and prevent you from making major purchases.

National Student Loan Data System (NSLDS)

If a student would like to check their Pell Grant and loan history, I encourage you to go onto https://nslds.ed.gov . The NSLDS is the Department of Education's database for federal student financial aid from schools, guaranty agencies, Direct Loan programs, and other Dept. of Ed programs. This will give you the access to review your overall financial aid.

Servicers

Servicers are the lenders who work out payment arrangements for student loans. You can go to www.studentloans.gov to research some. Some popular loan servicers are:

>Great Lakes www.mygreatlakes.org 1-800-236-4300
>
>Navient www.navient.com 1-800-722-1300
>
>FedLoan Servicing (PHEAA) myfedloan.org 1-800-699-2908
>
>Nelnet www.nelnet.com 1-888-486-4722
>
>MOHELA www.mohela.com 1-888-866-4352

Why Borrow at all?

I have spoken with many people about why students decide to take out loans. Especially when they borrow money when market estimates indicate that your particular major may not make enough money to pay back the loans in a reasonable time period. The ultimate answer? Because they can!

Often students take it upon themselves to take out a loan, without consulting a parent or guardian. If a student is eligible for loans, an institution must offer a student what they are eligible for. What makes a college loan interesting is that if a student wants a loan, all he or she needs to do is accept the loan offered, complete an entrance counseling, master promissory note (MPN), be at least a half time student, and he or she can receive the loan money! (PLUS Loans do not fall in this category).

Just think, if a regular person needs a loan, he/she would need to go to a bank, try to convince the Loan Officer that they need a loan, pass a credit check and show proof that he/she is employed. Once the bank receives the information and reviews it, they then decide whether they can trust you to repay the loan. A regular college student who is making Satisfactory Academic Progress (SAP) does not have to do any of this. Just think, who better than a young, naive college student who needs extra money to offer loans to. Be warned!

> *College is a business! For first generation college students, temptation will come in every corner. Be careful of the vultures that see you as prey and try to take advantage of you!*

Chapter 9

Seasons of Financial Aid

"When will refunds be disbursed?"

When someone mentions the seasons of the year, usually they are speaking of summer, winter, fall, and spring. Guess what? You can say the same thing when it comes to financial aid.

Before the semester starts and throughout the semester, there will be several times when the financial aid office is just packed! Students, parents, students' friends would be sitting down, standing up, leaning on the wall, sitting on the floor, or simply pacing the room, hoping to be the next person in line to speak with a financial aid counselor. Then again, there will be times when there's no one but the staff in the financial aid office. The timing of your visit makes all the difference. Consider: Why would you take a family vacation to Florida in June or July? The answer is because the kids are out of school. Most families would not take a week or two off with the kids when school is in session.

Here's something else to think about. Why is it that there are certain times in the semester that students may have to wait for two hours to see a financial aid counselor and then there are times when that same students may only have to wait ten seconds? Instead of me just giving you the answer, let me list the various financial aid seasons and explain each one.

Seasons

"Do I have Financial Aid" Season

When you think of the Fall, what comes to mind? Could it be football? Homecoming? Pre-K and K-12 students starting back at school? For colleges, it's the time to welcome brand new collegiate students who may have just graduated from high school, and time to welcome back returning students. Since we know that attending college is not free, let's call this season "Do I have Financial Aid?" Season." This season normally starts 2-3 months before a semester begins and the number of students and parents grows tremendously each week; especially, the week before and the week when the semester starts. While the "Do I have Financial Aid" Season can start in the Spring and Summer semesters too the Fall semester is usually the busiest.

During this season, the combination of recent high school graduates entering college for the first time, current students coming back from the summer break, students who are coming back to school after years away, transient students, transfer students, those who had not planned to go to college but suddenly decided to go, and those who were denied admission to their preferred college (so fall back on second and third choices) all coming at one time to see what it will take for them to get financial aid or find out the reason why they cannot receive financial aid.

The average wait time during this season could be 1-2 hours long. It's not intentional; it's just the volume of students to the financial aid offices increases. I receive complaints from students and from parents asking why it takes so long? Why are we slow? Why don't we hire more people?

My response: "Every student has a different issue or concern and each deserves to have their questions answered." I'm not trying to be a smart aleck, but when everyone comes in at the same time or waits until the last minute, instead of handling your business in a timely manner then you will just have to wait in those long lines. It is like Christmas. We all know that December 25 is Christmas day. So, when we shop at the last minute on December 23 or December 24, it shouldn't be a surprise when the lines are long and traffic is backed up for miles. I have often advised people to handle their FAFSA application and any other financial aid business up to 3 months before starting school. The last thing that you want to worry about when starting school is whether or not you have the money to go.

"Refund Check" Season

The next season, "Refund Check" Season, is as intense or possibly a little more intense because it involves direct money to the student. Students count on this money to pay bills, purchase a car, save, or spend it on whatever their hearts desire.

They can now afford whatever it is, just at that moment and they will use it. You can only imagine the intensity of the "Refund Check" season.

A refund check is any remaining money that is returned to the student after their tuition and any other debt accrued has been paid. The refund could be a physical check, or funds posted to a debit card, or deposited to your specified bank account. You will need to speak with your Student Accounts/Bursar's office to discuss how the school will issue the refund checks.

Let me give you an example. Your tuition for XYZ University is $2,250 and your book allowance is $1,000 for this semester.

You were awarded $3,048 for a Pell Grant and $1,000 from a scholarship this semester.

$2250 + $1,000 = $3,250 for your expenses

$3,048 + $1,000 = $4,048 for the money you received for the semester

$4,048 - $3,250 = **$798 is what you have left and that is the amount of your refund.**

Be careful though there may be times when a student is not eligible for a refund.

E.g.: Your tuition for XYZ University is $2,250 and housing is $10,000.

You were awarded $3,048 for a Pell Grant, $1000 for scholarship, $1,500 Subsidized loan, and $990 Unsubsidized loan.

$2250 + $10,000= $12, 250 for your expenses.

$3,048 + 1,000 + $1500 + 990= $6,538 for the money you received for this semester

If we do the math, $12,250- $6,538= **$5,712 which will be your remaining balance. This student and parent/guardian will need to discuss how the remaining balance will be paid. This student is not eligible for a refund.**

I'm not a licensed financial advisor so I cannot give you financial advice. What I can say is that, if I was in college today, I would really focus on my financial future, such as trying to retire by the age of 40. If financially feasible, I would take some of my refund (at least $1,000) and go to a local, federally insured bank (FDIC) and speak with a licensed financial advisor. I would look into investing the money in stocks so that while I'm in college my money would be working for me. College is a business, so act like it and make some money for myself too.

Many students will increase their credit hours in an effort to receive a bigger refund check. I advise students to know their limits. You might want more money in a refund check, but if you are not able to handle 9-12 credit hours and are failing classes, then clearly adding more classes is not the best choice. One of the worst things that you can do in college is to fail your classes and so not meet SAP. If you do not meet SAP in two consecutive semesters, you can lose your financial aid. If you do not have financial aid, then you will not receive funds to pay for your tuition and certainly cannot receive a refund check.

Many students will quit their jobs, become full-time students, and be dependent on their refund check to help with their financial situation. Bad idea! If a student's refund check is not what they anticipated and they need this money for their livelihood, they will stress themselves out and come into the financial aid office ready to curse someone out at eight in the morning!!

Speaking of stress, Refund season can be very stressful. I had several potential students who are said they were planning to attend college, who had never completed an admissions application and never completed a FAFSA application, but one of the first questions they would ask is, "How much money could I get for a refund check?" Of course, in my head, I was thinking, "so you're only going to school to receive a refund check? Not for an education or job advancement?" Clearly the answer to such questions could only be "yes."

Refunds can only be issued after the Add/Drop period ends. This is important to know because the Add/Drop period (usually the first week of classes) allows students to add a class (possibly incurring a late fee) or drop a class without any penalty. After the Add and Drop period ends, you are responsible for the classes you chose, and if you drop a class after the Add/Drop period ends it will count as a "Withdrawal" and charged to your account. At the close of the Add/Drop phase college can then pay your tuition and other collegiate debts. Once everything has been paid, you will be issued a refund check.

Let me point out an important fact that might be overlooked. In order for the student to receive a refund check, he/she must have some sort of financial aid that would cover your debt - tuition, fees, books, and for some students housing. You can't expect to have $1,000 in financial aid and $3,000 tuition and yet expect to get money back.

By the way, students can also lose their refund checks. As stated before, you must have some type of financial aid, scholarship, or loan that can cover the cost of your tuition and books. If you withdraw from all of your classes before your financial aid has been paid, then a refund would not be issued to you.

I can't tell you how many times that I've heard students yelling, crying, or screaming when they don't receive a refund check at a certain time period. The student will hit me with the, "Rent is due tomorrow" or "How am I going to pay my light bill?" I understand the importance of receiving money, but I always tell students that they must understand how to budget, prioritize, never wait until the last minute, understand their business, and not be scared to ask for help from family or friends.

"Withdrawal" Season

The next financial aid season is critical for students who are trying to protect their Grade Point Average (GPA), financial aid, or scholarship. Ladies and Gentlemen, let me introduce you to the "Withdrawal" season.

"If I was to withdraw from this class, how would it affect my financial aid?" This question is by far the most- asked question during this season. As a matter of fact it may be in my top five of all financial aid questions.

So, how did we get to the withdrawal season? Well, since the Add and Drop period is over, students who are not doing well in a class or have mistakenly taken the wrong class or don't like the professor have two choices: (1) Fail the Class or (2) Withdraw.

Failing a class is risky because it could affect their GPA and PACE ratio and SAP. Making less than a certain GPA can cause a student to lose their scholarship. For example, in Georgia there is a state scholarship that is funded by the state's lottery. The scholarship is called the HOPE Scholarship. To keep the HOPE Scholarship, the student must maintain a minimum GPA of 3.0. Since failing is not an option, the next best thing is for the student to withdraw from a class.

Before you withdraw, please speak with your financial aid representative FIRST. They should be able to review your status to see if withdrawing from a class would be Ok or if not, explain the consequences. Please don't ask a financial aid representative "What would you do?" or "Should I Withdraw?" Overall, this is a decision that you have to make. Our job is to inform you of your status and the potential consequences of your actions, When asked, "What would you do?" I don't know if my personal experience would be helpful. I had never withdrawn from a class. Even if I was not doing well, I just kept pushing and trying my best to get a decent grade. Of course, if a student took my advice and failed the class, they would want to blame me! But I was not the one who was making F's in the class and refusing to get help from a tutor and couldn't be bothered to go to the learning and tutoring center or was too busy to talk with my professor after class.

Withdrawing from all of your classes could be costly. If the financial aid paid for the student's tuition and the student needs/decides to withdraw from all of their classes, the financial aid office will perform a Title IV Calculation. Title IV Calculation (Return to Title IV/R2T4) requires the college or university to calculate the earned amount based on the last day of attendance of the semester. When a student who is receiving Title IV funding (Pell Grant, Subsidized Loan, Unsubsidized Loan) withdraws from all of their classes, the school must calculate the percentage of the period that was completed, based on class days attended. If the student withdraws from all of their classes before the 60% of their current semester has been completed, the school will bill the student. In other words, you will owe the school money.

Please read your college's withdrawal policy. Some schools only allow three withdraws overall and some may allow 6 withdraws overall. In addition, if you do withdraw, make sure to speak with someone in the Registrar's office to make sure that you have officially withdrawn from the class and get some written confirmation of that, if possible. I've known students who thought that they had withdrawn from a class but they were still registered for the class in the system. It's best to be safe and just check!

"Calm Before the Storm" Season

Once a student has received their refund check and has withdrawn from any class/classes that they don't want, the next season is the "Calm Before the Storm" season. This is the season when faculty or students wonder if the financial aid office is open because when they walk by the office there are no students lingering around. From dealing with some 300 students to being able to just breathe for a second, get lunch and even get mentally prepared for the next student or the next semester is a treat. For the majority of financial aid representatives, this is our favorite season.

Chapter 10

Satisfactory Academic Progress (SAP)

"The reason why your financial aid was denied is because you were not meeting SAP."

By now, you may be wondering about Satisfactory Academic Progress (SAP). Federal regulations require all students who are receiving Title IV financial aid funding to maintain **S**atisfactory **A**cademic **P**rogress in order to keep financial aid funding. Institutions that are receiving federal Title IV funding must make sure that students are progressing towards their degree and not being complacent. The federal government is not going to keep paying for a student to go to school if the student is not moving forward. It's like a job, an employer is not going to keep paying an employee if the employee does not work.

Title IV funding disbursements are through the Pell Grant, Subsidized Stafford Loans, Unsubsidized Stafford Loan, Parent Loan for Undergraduate Student (PLUS) loan, and Federal Work Study.

Per federal regulations it is mandated that the financial aid office monitor the academic progress of students. SAP is a financial aid policy. Please do not get it confused with University/College's academic probation policy.

Three factors that affect your SAP are:

(1) Grade Point Average (GPA)

(2) PACE ratio

(3) Maximum Timeframe

GPA (Grade Point Average)

A student must maintain a certain cumulative GPA based on the total credit hours they received. Below is an example.

Credit Hours	Cumulative GPA
0-12	1.5
13-27	1.65
28-36	1.75
37-59	1.85
60-90	2.00

At the end of each semester when grades have been posted and SAP has been reviewed, there is an expected cumulative minimum GPA that you must have in order to continue to receive your financial aid.

Pace Ratio

Pace is the percentage of attempted hours you pass while you are at the University/College. The Pace ratio for most universities is 66.66% you must pass at least 66% of the credit hours taken each semester in order to meet Pace On a job, if you are not meeting your quota, you may get a warning or close follow-up by your manager because you are falling short. If you continue to do poorly at your job, then you may find yourself without a job. Pace doesn't just look at one semester, it looks at all of your attempted hours and includes your transfer hours. In other words, if you are not doing well in school, the government is not going to continue to pay for your education.

> **Scenario**: A student was enrolled in 4 classes in the Fall 2021 semester. At the end of the semester, the student received the following grades: F, W, A, and B. Did the student meet PACE?
>
> **Answer:** No

Why? To be meeting PACE, you will have to be passing at least 66.66%. The student is at 50%.

Maximum Timeframe

All colleges have a limit on how many credit hours financial aid will pay. All financial aid recipients will be monitored and it's a requirement by the Department of Education. The goal is to make sure that each student is on the right path to graduate. Just so you know, if you are attending a junior college the attempted financial aid limit may be 90 credit hours. If you are at a four-year university, the attempted financial aid limit could be 180.

Let's say that you are attempted and passed 85 credit hours and you need 10 more credit hours to complete your degree.

Well, by the math, you know that you will be short by five credit hours. You can do a financial aid appeal and ask to be approved for the 10 additional hours that you need to graduate.

Students think that Withdrawals (W) do not hurt them. That may be true as regards to your GPA because the goal is to avoid grades that will lower your GPA but W's count as an attempt. So the more the W's you have, the less credit hours you have remaining. Let's look at the following example. Student has 85 attempted hours and he needs 10 more hours to complete his major. Let's say the student withdrew from four classes (3 credit hours each). If the student had not withdrawn from the classes, the student would have had the credit hours needed to have graduated.

Withdrawals are considered as attempts. Please speak with the Registrar's Office or an Academic Advisor in regards to how many withdrawals are allowed at your institution.

Scenario: Imagine that you are a student returning to a college that you once attended many years ago. In your head, you are thinking that you should be good because you are not the same, immature person that you were when you were 20. Now, you are 38 and more determined than ever to receive your degree. When you go to the financial aid department, they inform you that your financial aid has been denied. You think to yourself: "Why???" You haven't been in school in a while, and yet your financial aid is denied? The reason is because of SAP. Whether you have been out of school for 1, 5, 10, 20 years you must have been meeting the PACE ratio (passing rate of all the classes you attempted). Most schools require passing 66.66% of all classes and maintaining a certain grade point average (GPA).

Chapter 11

What is a Financial Aid Appeal?

"How can I get my financial aid back?"

From academic to judiciary, there are many forms of appeals at the tertiary level. For the purposes of this book; however, we are only focusing on financial aid appeals. A financial aid appeal is a petition/request/plea to get your financial aid back. You may have been denied aid for many reasons - from not meeting SAP or that you have used up all your attempted hours and in order to move forward, you need approval to receive funding for a few additional hours. Your college Academic Adviser can assist students in filling out an academic plan that shows which specific classes you plan to take and when. Please note this plan must come from the Academic Advisor, not your professor or a representative in another department, but your Academic Advisor. The Academic Advisor will give a student specific guidance on the classes that they need to take to graduate. The Academic Advisor typically signs the Academic Plan or approves it with a rubber stamp.

A college does not have to allow an appeal. You are not entitled to be granted an appeal and many appeals are denied.

In addition to an Academic Plan, you may want to consider including documents that could be used to support your request.

Supporting Documents/Mitigating Circumstances

If you have to submit a financial aid appeal I suggest that students also submit supporting documents that provide proof and help explain how the personal issues you experienced affected you and caused you to do poorly in your classes. In other words, there were mitigating circumstances – situations beyond your control that financial aid investigators can readily understand why you would be negatively affected. Examples of supporting documents that provide proof of mitigating circumstances that can help your appeal are medical records, police reports, doctors' notes- with their signature, letters (preferably on letterheads) from directors of homeless shelters- with their signature-, divorce decree, and obituaries or funeral bulletins of deceased family members.

Approach the appeal as if you were going to court – a person can say this happened and that happened or present written explanations but without documents to prove your claim, that will not help you. The process has been abused by too many students and parents who would lie or manipulate a story in an effort to win back their financial aid and so no longer accepts just the student's explanation of mitigating circumstances. This is why documentation and proof of the circumstances is very critical.

I have had students who were upset that they were asked to provide financial or personal information when completing their financial aid SAP appeal. Many students feel that the school is being nosy, and it is none of the school's business. The truth of the matter is that if you do not want to provide such information to receive funds then you can always pay out of pocket. Even if you opted to participate in a payment plan personal financial information would still be required. Don't forget, college is a business.

Warning

If you did not meet SAP in a semester, the financial aid office will put you on a warning or probationary status. Look at the warning status as strike 2 in baseball. A letter will be mailed to you or an email sent to you at your school email address. While you are on warning status, you will be eligible to receive financial aid funding; however, if you do not meet SAP the following semester then you can lose your financial aid and will have to complete a financial aid SAP Appeal.

> **Scenario:** It is hard to imagine, but I often hear from students who feel that it is not fair that they lost their financial aid because of SAP or that their appeal to reinstate their financial aid was denied. This is just ridiculous to me that they did not perform well in their classes, but they are

frustrated with us. I like to use examples, so I usually give a student this example.

Think of financial aid like your girlfriend. You finally meet the woman of your dreams. You've been waiting 12 years (high school) to meet her. Now, since you got your girlfriend, named Financial Aid, you do not take care of her. When you should be studying, you are out partying with other people or maybe working those long hours, and do not do your homework nor prepare yourself for class. The only thing on your mind is that refund check from her and so in that first semester, you did poorly; from withdrawing (W) to receiving F's in your class. You received a notice that you were placed on warning, but you did not take it seriously. Your sweetheart gave you an ultimatum. The next semester, you told yourself you would do your best, but that thought was quickly erased and you kept skipping out of assignments and tutorials. Since you were in warning, you did not want to withdraw because that would surely lower your PACE ratio. At the end of the semester, you did not do well in your classes and you lose your financial aid. In time, you find it hard to save up for school. You wanted to participate in the payment plan option, but did not have enough money to pay bills and school at the same time. The money that you did have saved from your refund checks, you used it to buy a new car. Hoping to get her back, you complete a financial aid appeal. Weeks go by, no news from the financial aid office. You storm in, very upset with financial aid representatives who have not given you a report, but not mad at yourself for not handling your business.

In life, there is something called cause and effect. When it comes to your assignments, you are responsible for them. Not taking care of your business will affect your standings with being able to have financial aid. It should not take for you to lose your financial aid to finally start caring about it.

Professional Judgment

In life we know that at times it can seem unfair, biased, and disappointing, wishing things would go as easy as saying 1, 2, and 3. Many times there are situations that are out of our control and would make it hard for us to move forward toward our goal. To illustrate, dependent students need their parents' information while completing the FAFSA. What if their parents are deceased or nowhere to be found? Without their parent's information, the FAFSA would be considered incomplete. One thing that students can do is to complete an appeal for a Professional Judgment. Professional Judgment gives special authority to a financial aid administrator (typically a manager) to adjust the data from the FAFSA by overriding a student's dependent status if a student has a certain situation that needs immediate review (e.g.: if dependent student's parents are deceased and student is an orphan, or dependent student is homeless).

The financial aid administrator does not have the power to change the need analysis formula or make adjustments to the

EFC; however, the school can adjust inputs to the formula. The changes to this financial aid file are dictated by the impact of the special circumstances on the family's income and assets. Once the new data information has been added to the standard formula, a new EFC figure will emerge.

Professional Judgment decisions vary and are not always guaranteed to be in favor of the student. If you must request a Professional Judgment, please remember to bring in supporting documents. Again, like going to court, you must have proof to validate the truth of what you are saying.

Chapter 12

Parent and Child (Student) Relationship

"I hate that I can't get the Pell Grant because of my parents. They have the money! I don't! I don't even live with them. I pay my own rent and bills. Just because I'm under 24 years old, I'm stuck with dealing with my parents! I hate that!"

I want to dedicate a chapter to the parent-child (student) relationship. One of the biggest complaints I hear from parents and students is the fact that a student (dependent) cannot receive financial aid without their parent's information. From the parent(s) point of view, if their child can go serve in the military at the age of 18, buy alcohol at the age of 21, purchase a gun at the age of 21, and can go out and vote at the age of 18, clearly they should be able to register for financial aid without burdening them for their information. In some students' point of view, if they pay their own bills, have their own place, or if they are not getting along with parents, why do they still need to be attached to their parent? This is even more inexplicable if the parent makes a substantial amount of money that clearly disqualifies the student for receiving the Pell Grant (free money). Leaving the student only eligible for a loan. I usually explain to students and parents that there is no way around this requirement and that the only way to change it is to write to their Congressional Representatives and Senators and tell them how they feel and urge changes to the legislation. I have never met one parent or student who has ever done so.

Parents, unless your child is married or over 24 years of age, they will need your information to complete the FAFSA. If not, as I stated before, the student's FAFSA will be considered incomplete and rejected.

Below are responses to a few questions that I have been asked several times.

> **When a parent puts their information on the FAFSA, does the FAFSA do a credit check?**
>
> *No, once you complete the FAFSA, there will be no credit check. There will be a social security check to make sure that you are the right person. The only time there will be a credit check for the parent is if they apply to participate in the PLUS loan.*
>
> **If a parent is a student, do they have to complete another FSA ID for their child?**
>
> *No.*
>
> **Instead of the child's biological parent(s), can a Grandparent or Aunt/Uncle complete the FAFSA under the parent section and then electronically sign it?**

No. The FAFSA requires information from the biological parent. If a person were awarded legal guardianship of the child, by the courts then they would be able to sign the FAFSA.

What if a parent's income changes from the tax information used in the FAFSA application? Can the parent do an appeal?

Yes, a parent can request an appeal (Professional Judgment). This is important because a major factor that determines your EFC is family income. If you have a very high income, then you may not be eligible for Pell and the only type of financial aid that you may be eligible for is an unsubsidized loan. For example, in 2019 the parent was making $95,000 and then their company laid them off. It's now 2021, and you are either still unemployed or making about $20,000. That's a dramatic life change that with necessary proof would probably result in an appeal being approved.

If a student's financial aid has been denied because of SAP, could the student still qualify for the PLUS loan?

No. If the student is not meeting SAP, they lose all of the benefits and privileges from financial aid.

If the student or parent pays out of pocket for student's tuition and later on they complete the

FAFSA, could the student or parent be reimbursed?

Yes, the student or parent can receive a reimbursement if they are eligible. In receiving the reimbursement (and refund), many schools give you the option to have the money to be deposited directly in to your bank account or onto a bankcard. Just keep in mind that many schools have deadlines for when they can distribute reimbursements and refunds. My advice: take care of your FAFSA way before the semester begins.

Can a student be awarded financial aid at two schools at the same time?

No. Federal regulations forbid a student to be awarded financial aid at two schools at the same time.

Conflicts

When I first began my financial aid career, I used to have parents who would come into my office and refuse to help their child and I have dealt with students who would come into my office, frustrated because their parent(s) did not want anything to do with helping them get into college. It didn't matter that the student (their child), needed their information to complete the FAFSA. The parent refused to help.

Over time, and after speaking with many students and parents, I had to learn that there are several sides to a story. You have the student's version, the parent's version, and the overall truth. From my observation most parents want the best for their child but they do not trust their child or see a lack of efforts by the child that affects their relationship. In the eyes of the students, many students are fed up with their parents for not taking care of their responsibilities leaving the child to wish they were an independent student.

Trust and Lack of Effort

In regards to trust, most parents trust their child to do the right thing. Many parents have supported their child's dreams and goals. Sadly however, many students have done things in the past that left their parents with disappointment and mistrust. I had a parent to come into my office to argue about why their child's SAP Appeal was denied. While the parent was speaking, I kept staring at the student expecting him to speak up. Since he refused to talk, I had to inform the parent that since the child started college, he had continuous bad grades. I informed the parent that if she needed additional confirmation about her child's poor academic performance then she should have the child (student) sign a FERPA form (that would allow professors and others to speak with her and give detailed information about her son). Yes, I know it sounds like I was speaking to a student who is in high school, but some parents need to see how their child is actually doing academically; especially when the student is telling their parent that they are doing well in school or that the financial aid department is bullying them.

Today, there are so many opportunities for students, but many parents don't understand why their child lacks drive and instead want to blame everything on society. Some parents get upset because their child doesn't complete the FAFSA or fill out scholarship applications, which the parent then does for the student instead of making the student do it themselves or face the consequences.

Not Handling Their Responsibility

Since we discussed the issues that some parents have with their children (students), it's only fair to mention the issues that some students have with their parents.

Students complain incessantly and wish that the financial aid laws would change because their parents are not taking care of their responsibilities and dependent students are seriously affected.

Regardless of the fact that the student pays their own bills or does not live with their parent(s), they will still need their parents' information to complete their FAFSA. Being a dependent student can be a burden because students rely heavily on their parents to provide them with information so they can complete the application. What's worse is that for many students, the only financial aid that they can receive is a loan because of high parental income

Another common issue is when the student has to constantly wait on their parents to give them their tax information There have been times when parents came to my office to ask for an extension for their child's financial aid or ask what they could do to hold their classes. Yes, there are times when you may understand why a parent's taxes were not complete. For example, someone stealing your identify and illegally using their social security number. Since financial aid offices are now able to use tax information from two years before Prior Prior Year, taxes should have been completed two years ago and so eliminate any excuses of why a student has not completed their financial aid application. Unfortunately, that's not always the case. The student would be in my office frustrated, trying to figure out a plan to receive financial aid without having to deal with their parent.

The purpose of this section is to highlight trust and communication issues between parents and their college students. Both have understandable points and I don't have an answer to solve all the problems. I just know this, that when parents and students work together, as one unit, trusting each other, that this can go a long way in improving relationships and making sure that mutual goals are reached.

Chapter 13

International Students
"How can I get into college?"

Getting an opportunity to receive an education is not just an American ambition as many students from other countries come to the United States to receive an education. They do so to help their families here in the United States or in their home country. Many students who want to attend college have asked me how they can go do so. The first step is to speak with an Admissions Representative to find out about all the documents that are required to enter a particular college. I would also advise international students (especially first time college students) to visit the International Admissions office on that campus. In addition, research various organizations and programs on campus that can help international students.

If you are not born in the United States, be prepared to turn in such documentation as your green card or a Certificate of Naturalization that shows that you are a citizen. Please make sure that none of your documents are expired. In order to be accepted at a college, a student who is not from this country who is selected for verification will need to provide proper paperwork to prove their citizenship. Once a student submits the documents, the college will have to get the information verified by the Department of Homeland Security.

In the United States, if you are a male student who is between the ages of 18 and 25, you must register for the Selective Service. If you are an international male student who was over age 26 when you came into the United States, you can use the passport from your country to prove that you came into this country over the age of 26 years old and that you do not have to register for selective service. The Passport has the stamp that shows the date when you entered the United States of America.

If you do not speak English well or you do not understand the terms, I strongly recommend that get help from someone who understands the English language - verbal and written so no one can take advantage of you. Colleges want to make sure that you clearly understand all questions and find out how to help you.

Please take note: You must be a citizen, permanent resident or eligible non-citizen in order to receive financial aid If you received a bachelor's degree in the USA or any other country, you are not eligible to receive the Pell Grant. If you are designated as an international student you will not be eligible for financial aid based programs and I would encourage you to seek scholarships and loans.

Chapter 14

Top of the Mountain

"Thank you for helping me out."

I am hoping that by this time you are feeling confident about financial aid, as if you are "on top of the mountain." More importantly, that you now have a better understanding of your personal financial aid and the realization that college is a business. I would have to agree with those who say that financial aid is not an easy subject to understand. Working with many students, parents, teachers, faculty, and staff to answer the tough and sometimes confusing questions inspired me to write this book. The book's mission is to give you insights and information that hopefully have eliminated some of your frustration and fear, and educated you on some key steps, things not to do, and the reasons why.

If you are serious about going to college, current and future students should:

1. Understand your own reasons and motivation for getting a degree.

2. Stay focused and remember why you are going to college.

3. Surround yourself with positive, like-minded people.
4. Do not be afraid to ask for help or ask questions. Asking questions is encouraged.
5. The more that you know and understand, the bigger advantage you will have towards reaching your goals.
6. To reach a goal, you must be disciplined.
7. If you are not serious about going to college, don't waste other people's time nor the federal government's money.
8. If you keep looking back at your past, it will be hard for you to look forward to your future.
9. No one can keep you from your goals but you.
10. You, as a student should make it your own responsibility to take the time to learn about financial aid. Do not just leave it to your parent!
11. Know and understand the financial aid and admission process, what classes you need to take for your major, and the type of career and salary that your major can provide.
12. Know and understand the market you want to go into
13. College is not going to teach you everything you need to know. You may have to do additional research for yourself on the career you hope to follow.
14. College is a business, so prepare and react accordingly.

15. Relationships are vital - not just with your professors but with your classmates as well.

16. Create a vision board to show what you want to accomplish and who you would like to meet.

17. There may be times when your parents or friends may not understand your vision but if it's your dream, pursue it with passion.

18. Learn and understand what separates you from everyone else.

19. Your experience can go a long way. Look into co-ops or internships regardless of whether the positions are paid or not.

20. Before you make any major decisions weigh the pros and cons. Write them out on a sheet of paper so you can actually see the differences.

21. Find something that will inspire you when you are feeling down. If you are tired of having loans and the thought of paying them back frustrates you, do well in your classes so that you can apply for various scholarships or grants. The better your grades are in college, the greater the opportunity for you to receive scholarships.

22. A closed mouth doesn't get fed. In other words, if you don't talk to a wide range of people then you will never know about unpublished opportunities. In addition to the scholarship department on your campus, ask your

professors, department chairs, people at your job, fraternities, sororities, your insurance company, and other companies if they know of, or are providing scholarships or grants.

23. I hope you believe, as I do, that when God closes a door, he always opens a window. Look for the good and stay positive!

Chapter 15

Key Terms
"Can you please explain this to me?"

Throughout this book, there have been several key terms that I consider highly important for learning about the financial aid process. Let's review some of these key terms.

6 -Month Grace Period- For six months after graduating or after you stop attending college, you do not have to make any payments on your loans. After this grace period, a student is expected to contact a servicer and begin making payments on the loan.

Add/Drop Period- A fixed period of time (usually the first week of classes) during which a student can add (or drop) a class.

Consortium Agreement- An agreement or contract between two colleges/universities (home school and host school) that acknowledges your registration at both schools for financial aid and credit purposes. Only your home school can administer your financial aid from Title IV and state awards.

Default- If you accepted a federal student loan in college then finished school or stopped attending and after your 6-month Grace Period, you do not make a payment for 270 days, then you would be penalized for refusing to pay back a federal government loan. You would have failed to meet your obligation, broken your promise to pay to pay back the loan and tagged as defaulting on the loan. Once you are in default, you cannot receive any type of financial aid until your debt has been paid or you have satisfied a payment plan option.

Dependent Student- Students who are under 24 years old and need their parents' information to complete the FAFSA.

EFC - Estimated Family Contribution-a projection of how much money a student's family might be responsible for their college education. This is based on information on the FAFSA from the parent and student (if the student is a dependent student). This estimate would include household size, income, assets, participation in free and reduced price school lunch, if you are a dislocated worker, the number of people in your household and those who are attending college. When it comes to your Pell Grant, your EFC will determine how much free money from you can be awarded.

Entrance Counseling- An activity that educates the borrower (student) on budgeting and finance.

Exit Counseling- Completed when you graduate, stop attending college, or you go below the halftime status. The purpose of the exit counseling is to educate students on repayment options and to remind students that they have a loan that they must pay back.

FAFSA-Free Application for Federal Student Aid - an application to receive financial aid for college.

FERPA - Family Educational Rights and Privacy Act - Federal law that protects the privacy of student education records. The law applies to all schools that receive funds from the U.S Department of Education.

Financial Aid Appeal- A student has lost their financial aid by not meeting SAP or needing additional financial aid and will need to complete a SAP Appeal form/document along with having an Academic Plan from an Academic Adviser. In many cases, supporting documents are required.

FSA ID- Username and password that can give a person access to their federal student aid information online and can be used as an official signature.

Grade Point Average (GPA)- Measurement of students' class performance and academic achievement.

In-School Deferment- Tool to postpone payment on loans you accepted at a school you previously attended until after you are finished at the school in which you are currently enrolled.

Institutional Student Informational Record (ISIR)- Data that is transmitted to a college/university from the Department of Education. This information comes from the FAFSA.

Independent Student- Students who do not need their parents' information when completing a FAFSA. Criteria for designation as an independent student: at least 24 years old; have a child and be able to prove that they are receiving half of their financial support; be an active duty military personnel. If the student is under 25 and wishes to be designated as an Independent student they must be married or separated; both parents are deceased.

Lender- Loan company, public or private, that lends money and usually collects interest.

Loans- Money that is borrowed from private or federal sources to be used for college and to be repaid once a student has graduated stopped attending college.

Master Promissory Note (MPN) - A contract that states that the student owes a loan and is expected to make a repayment.

Maximum Time Frame- Colleges have a limit on how many credit hours financial aid will pay. All financial aid recipients will be monitored and it's a requirement by the Department of Education monitors

NSLDS -National Student Loan Database System) - The U.S Department of Education's database of students' financial aid history.

Pace Ratio- Pass/Fail ratio that must exceed 66.66% in order for students to continue to receive financial aid.

Parent Loan for Undergraduate Student (PLUS Loan) - Title IV loan for which a parent can apply for their child (Dependent Student). For this loan, the parent would undergo a credit check. If the parent is approved, the parent can take on the responsibility of the loan; however, if the parent is the denied, the student can receive an additional unsubsidized loan.

Pell Grant- Title IV free money that only eligible students may receive after completing the FAFSA. These funds do not have to be repaid.

Prior Prior Year- Students and parents can report their taxes from two years ago (prior-prior year) on the FAFSA application.

Professional Judgment (PJ)- Professional Judgment gives special authority to a financial aid administrator (typically a manager) to make adjustments to the data from the FAFSA by overriding a student's dependent status.

SAP-Satisfactory Academic Progress: Policy that evaluates the student's grade point average (GPA), pace ratio, and maximum time frame to ensure that the student is being successful in college.

SAR- Student Aid Report: Information that the student receives when they submit their FAFSA. The data that is listed on the SAR will be used to determine a student's financial aid award.

Servicers- Company that will handle your loan repayments and will work with you on various payment options.

Subsidized Loan- The government will pay the interest on the loan.

Title IV funding- Money that the federal government will provide to colleges and universities. It includes funding for the Pell Grant, Subsidized Loans, Unsubsidized Loans, and Federal Work Study.

Transient Student- While enrolled in one college, the student is temporarily attending another college.

Tuition- The cost of attending classes at a college or university.

Unsubsidized Loan- The student is responsible for paying the interest of the loan.

Verification- Requested document(s) that can confirm various information that was reported on the FAFSA or updated information.

Withdrawal- A time after the Add/Drop period when the student can cancel their registration for a class. The penalty for a withdrawal is that your class will count as an attempt and be recorded as a W on your permanent record. Depending on your SAP status a withdrawal can hurt your Pace Ratio and lead to a loss of your financial aid.

References

Georgetown University Center on Education and the Workforce, The College Payoff: Education, Occupations, Lifetime Earnings. Anthony P. Carnevale, Stephen J. Rose, and Ban Cheah.

College Board Advocacy and Policy Center: Five Ed Ways Pays. www.collegeboard.org. 2011

Family Educational Rights and Privacy Act (FERPA). U.S Department of Education.
https://www2.ed.gov/policy/gen/guid/fpco/ferpa/index.html?src=rn

Federal Student Aid. FAFSA: Apply for Aid
https://studentaid.ed.gov/sa/fafsa

Federal Student Aid. FAFSA: Apply for Aid

https://studentaid.ed.gov/sa/fafsa/filling-out/dependency

National Association of Student Financial Aid Administrators.
https://www.nasfaa.org/ppyresources

About the Author

Trae D. Johnson: son of Jimmie Johnson and the late Essie L. Johnson, and the youngest of three, is a native of Harlem, Georgia. He is married to LaToya B. Johnson.

Trae is a published author. His debut paperback, "Family Scars," a fiction novel, was released in 2020. Trae is a fiction and non-fiction writer. In his background, Trae has ten years of financial aid and higher education experience, 19 years of leadership experience and non-profit experience. Currently Trae is a Student Financial Services Counselor at a major college in Georgia. In 2015, he was nominated and selected as the Outstanding Staff of the Year. He is a member of Phi Beta Sigma Fraternity, Inc. and one of the charter members of the Sigma Eta Sigma Chapter. Trae has won numerous awards from his fraternity including: State of GA Chapter President of the year twice and the R.O Sutton State Executive Board Member of the year award and is a Registered Parliamentarian. He is a member of the Dogwood Unit-National Association of Parliamentarians. Trae has participated in many outreach events, educating students at local high schools on the importance of going to college, volunteering at numerous back-to-school drives, presenting workshops at leadership conferences, and participating on panel discussions for college awareness programs.

Trae is a big Atlanta sports fan. He loves the Atlanta Hawks, Atlanta Falcons, and Atlanta United. When he is not writing, Trae enjoys listening to music especially New Edition, Outkast, Eightball & MJG, Luke, Keith Sweat, Jay-Z, Babyface, Master P and No Limit, Michael Jackson, and Bobby Brown.

For more information about the author and on his upcoming publications please go to his website at www.traejohnson.com.

www.ingramcontent.com/pod-product-compliance
Lightning Source LLC
Chambersburg PA
CBHW071859070526
44583CB00016B/1758